Praise for The Way Ahead

Controversial and passionate, *The Way Ahead* chall␣␣␣␣␣␣␣␣␣ple of God to seek unity in and beyond the norms of dogma and ␣␣␣␣␣ny – to step out in faith and courageously grasp this new time. Ian Fraser touches the edge of excitement and newness in an earthy, scholarly and profound way. His life quest for integration flows through this book.

Sister Christine Anderson, FCJ, Craighead Institute

My first encounter with Ian Fraser was in the early days of Scottish Churches House in the 1960s when he sought to earth his vision of ecumenism in the pioneering work of the House. This book continues to challenge the church's thinking. He reaffirms that vision of Christian unity as about the world's needs and not simply an exercise in 'ecclesiastical joinery'; and he calls us to see ministry as the task of the whole people of God, not reserved to the few. At a time when it is too easy for the church to retreat into some pietistic huddle, Ian reminds us of the mission imperative which takes the world seriously; and moreover, he writes with a sense of hope and expectation.

Bishop Bruce Cameron, former Primus of the Scottish Episcopal Church

Dr Ian Fraser is a treasure trove of biblical scholarship, wisdom and common sense. *The Way Ahead* draws on a lifelong and worldwide experience of Christian communities 'on the edge'. With inspirational hope, Ian Fraser points to a bright and valid future for the church, shorn of ecclesiastical irrelevances. It is a prophetic vision that cheers the heart. It will not meet with universal approval – but then you know what they say about prophets in their own country (and in their own time!).

Tom Fleming, Radio and television broadcaster

Drawing on a vast storehouse of knowledge, experience, insight and anecdote, Ian Fraser raises fundamental questions concerning the mission and ministry of the whole people of God. In ecumenical discussions so often these perspectives are referred to briefly and concentrated discussion focuses on the ordained ministry – to the detriment of the witness of the church and ecumenical rapprochement. This is a stimulating and challenging book.

Dr Alan Falconer, minister of St Macher Cathedral, Aberdeen, formerly Director of the Faith and Order Commission of the World Council of Churches

THE WAY AHEAD:
GROWN-UP CHRISTIANS

IAN M. FRASER

THE WAY AHEAD:

GROWN-UP CHRISTIANS

IAN M. FRASER

WILD GOOSE PUBLICATIONS

Copyright©Ian M Fraser2006.

Published by Wild Goose Publications
Fourth Floor, Savoy House, 140 Sauchiehall Street, Glasgow G2 3DH
Wild Goose Publications is the publishing division of The Iona Community
Scottish Charity No. SC003794 Limited Company Reg. No. SC096243
ISBN 1-905010-25-7
13-digit ISBN: 978-1-905010-25-7

Distributed in Australia and New Zealand by Willow Connection Pty Ltd,
Unit 7A, 3–9 Kenneth Road, Manly Vale NSW 2093.
Permission to reproduce any part of this work in Australia or New Zealand
should be sought from Willow Connection.

A Catalogue record for this book is available from the British Library.

Printed by Bell & Bain, Thornliebank, Glasgow

In appreciation of my sister Margaret,
and of Jack and Janet Orr, pioneers

Brothers and sisters, stop thinking like children.
Be infants in evil but in your mental outlook be adults.

1 Corinthians 14:20

CONTENTS

The priesthood of all believers, the ministry of the whole people of God, has been a lifetime's work and an enduring passion for Ian Fraser, and, in this, he has been an encouragement and inspiration for Christians of many traditions. *The Way Ahead* tells the story of some communities which have lived out this ministry, often in very difficult circumstances, and explores ways in which the church of the twenty-first century might rise to the challenge of mature, ecumenical discipleship. At a time when Christianity often seems to be fragmenting into ideological sectarianism, this book, with its emphasis on practice, is a timely and helpful contribution.

Kathy Galloway, April 2006

INTRODUCTION

Dear Reader,

I have a concern which I would like to share with you.

The word 'ecumenical' seems to make people's minds fly to the notion of churches bent on unity. That is a valid but secondary use of the word. The Greek *oikoumene* stands for 'the whole inhabited earth'. Fourteen uses in the New Testament are simply translated 'world'. Ecumenical commitment focuses not on the church but on the world God so loved that he sent his Son. The church then comes in as an agent of that love. Church unity must be shaped so as to forward God's will for the unity of the world in justice, truth and peace. Otherwise it may be self-serving.

I have tried to express this in the words of a prayer:

Lord Christ, forbid us unity
which leaves us where we are and as we are:
welded into one company but extracted from the battle,
engaged to be yours but not found at your side …

To be engaged with Jesus Christ in transforming the world implies a ministry. In the New Testament there is only one definitive ministry alongside his, that of the whole church. To build up the church for its life and mission, gifts of the Spirit are distributed among God's people. These gifts form bases for particular ministries which contribute to the total ministry. They are given to equip the church membership for its work. More official forms of ministry must never take over, as if they stand for the ministry that matters (though the history of the church has thrown up plenty of examples of this defect):

'He (Christ) gave gifts that some would be apostles, some prophets, some evangelists, some pastors and teachers, to equip the saints for the work of ministry, for building up the body of Christ – until all of us come to the unity of the faith and of the knowledge of the Son of God, to maturity, to the measure of the stature of the fullness of Jesus Christ.' (Ephesians 4:1–13)

Official forms of ministry should have an auxiliary, enabling character, not a dominating one. Those who would exercise the ministry committed to all the followers of Jesus Christ are called to put their gifts to use. Only thus can members become grown-up, able to contribute a telling service in and to the world. In his letters to the churches Paul keeps urging Christians not to remain infants in faith. The world has to be turned around to evidence God's good will for its life. That calls for investment by adult Christians.

The Ephesians passage goes on:

'We must no longer be children, tossed to and fro and blown about by every wind of doctrine, by people's trickery, by their craftiness and deceitful scheming. But speaking the truth in love, we must grow up in every way into him who is the Head, into Christ – from whom the whole body, joined and knitted together by every ligament with which it is equipped, as each part is working properly, promotes the body's growth in building itself up in love.'

This is the ecumenical challenge.

1.

THE CHURCH COMMUNITY IN MINISTRY

A FAVOURABLE TIME

In every age we are faced with the determination of God to transform all created life in justice, truth and peace.

In every age we are faced with the deliberate self-limitation of God through the choice of human beings to be partners in that work of transformation.

When the time was ripe Jesus Christ came, in a fully human life. He came among us as *arabon*: 'the colour of God's money staked in a gambler's throw for a new world'. He announced and represented God's Kingdom: the whole fabric of created life working God's way. He called people to join him in this work. From those who responded, church was formed.

The Kingdom must be prayed for and worked for – and also, in the end, be received as a gift: 'Fear not, little flock – it is your Father's good pleasure to give you the Kingdom.'

The church, on the other hand, must be built up, each limb and organ contributing to the life of the body whose Head is Jesus Christ. To be effective in ministering with him to the world God loves, it must 'grow up into him', becoming equipped for the job, all its gifts being exercised with ever greater maturity.

The church in the West is experiencing what Isaiah called 'a time of God's favour'. What look to be drawbacks hold promise:

a) The church is no longer the power in the land that it once was. It can no longer set itself up as the authorised dispenser of God's judgments on people and events. It is no longer listened to just because it is church. So it is in a better position to give heed to the words of Jesus about power. Faced with a bid by the mother of James and John to give them a privileged position, Jesus warned: 'You know that, with the Gentiles, rulers lord it over their subjects and the great make their authority felt. That must not be your way! With you whoever wants to be great must serve, and whoever wants to be first must be the slave of all: as the Son of Man came not to be served but to serve and to give his life a ransom for many.'

In his letters to the Corinthians Paul insists that it is the weak things which overthrow the mighty; and that, in his own case, it is when he is weak that he is strong. Jesus Christ, treated as a nothing, crucified, risen, testified to the effectiveness of a different power from that wielded by those with clout in the land. Dietrich Bonhoeffer put the matter succinctly and brilliantly. Christians are called to 'participation in the powerlessness of God in the world'.[1]

b) The church in the West is being pruned back. What seems negative has positive implications. Jesus warned disciples that they had to be prepared for times of pruning. He identified himself as the Vine and his Father as the Vinedresser. He told them that they, as branches, would be subjected to the cutting away of dead wood and of spurs which were no longer productive. This was needed to achieve greater fruitfulness, a more abundant harvest.

c) The church in our time is more alert to the danger of becoming what Swiss basic Christian communities called a *Kuschelgruppe* – a 'cuddling group', absorbed in itself. Yet the media so often measure the church's health as if it existed by and for itself. As football support is measured by numbers going through the turnstiles, so the yardstick for church commitment has been taken to be numbers turning up at a building. How can that be the means of assessing the vitality of a community which is to be like leaven changing solid dough to produce bread, like salt giving life savour, like light active to chase away darkness? As well attempt, by eye measurement, to distinguish the water from the whisky in a dram! The service of the church is to get lost in creative self-giving, that the world be transformed in justice, truth and peace.

Some years ago I visited Fuller Theological Seminary in California. Students approached me with words emblazoned on T-shirts: 'Don't Go To Church'. When I looked after them I read on the back: 'Be The Church'.

I was in London when Bob Geldof and others summed up the efforts to release poor countries from crippling debt. There Gordon Brown paid tribute to the church and other religious bodies for providing dynamic at the heart of the movement. When a quarter of a million people marched against the Iraq war where was the church? In the thick of things, not separately labelled. Faslane protests, G8 summit pressures, the Make Poverty History campaign had Christians at their heart. Veteran Labour politician Roy Hattersley has confessed, as an atheist, that the evidence is compelling that caring friendship for the old, the weak, the vulnerable in our society would be substantially missing were Christians not bedded into local situations, acting there with enlightened compassion.

Might there come a day when the media, armed with greater perceptiveness than is provided by the number of bums on pews, learn to look on this time as signalling a high point in the church's life?[2]

The calling of the church is to be part of the human struggle for justice, truth and peace: to give that struggle heart and hope through the gospel without looking for credit for itself. The credit for a transformed world is to be God's.

It is difficult to read the signs of one's own time. In the West, are we at a time of a decline in Christian belief? I think that there is a chance that we are in Kingdom territory where humanity is shouldering church to the side – not rejecting it but giving it its true servant place – in favour of direct Kingdom priorities.

What makes church church has to be continually discovered. What exists has to be continually reshaped. Jeremiah provides an illuminating illustration. He is told to go down to the potter's house. He finds the potter working at his wheel. Jeremiah is instructed by what he sees.

The vessel he was making of clay was spoiled in the potter's hand.
He reworked it into another vessel as seemed good to him.
Then the word of the Lord came to me: 'Can I not do with you,
O house of Israel, just as the potter has done?' says the Lord. (Jeremiah 18:4–5)

The basic material is not discarded. It is reshaped. In the reshaping the original intention may be better realised – even improved upon when fresh imaginative possibilities are brought to bear.

If I find that some people are giving up on church, I do not try to dissuade them. Their action may cause the church, as a prodigal, to come to itself. But I do urge them to get together with others to bring a small community into being and to join them on a journey of discovery about life's meaning and purpose.

Something like this is what had happened when my wife, Margaret, and I participated in the first European Congress of Basic Christian Communities in Holland in 1983. The congress lasted for four days. For three of these, those who came from outside Holland were allocated to different basic Christian communities to share life experiences. Our group, the Salland group, had come about in the following way. One person had contacted a few acquaintances and had put an advert in the local paper to this effect: 'I want to find what it is to live the Christian faith today. It seems to me that the official church is hindering rather than helping me. Any others willing to join me in this quest?' In no time thirty people had responded. By the time we arrived the number had risen to over seventy. Two small communities had to be formed to cater effectively for those keen to go on such a pilgrimage.

THE CHURCH'S MINISTRY – INTEGRATED OR FRACTURED

Community and separateness

The Greek word *aphorizo* is used in contrasting senses in the New Testament. These illuminate behaviour which is appropriate and inappropriate in light of the gospel. The core meaning concerns the setting of boundaries. This can be done so as to strengthen or fragment community.

a) At the beginning of Acts 13 we are told that, in Antioch, prophets and teachers had been fasting, open to the Holy Spirit. The message came to them: 'Separate off Barnabas and Saul for the work I want them to do.' The work is not identified. The boundary markers placed along the way will be there to keep them on track. How this works out is made clear in Acts 16. Paul and his companions are forbidden by the Holy Spirit to preach the Word in the province of Asia. (How many evangelists are sufficiently open to the Holy Spirit to be prepared to hear that at times they should just shut up and stay available?) Passing through Phrygia and Galatia they attempt to go into Bithynia, but again the Holy Spirit bars the way. They either skirt Mysia or go straight through to Troas. There the man from Macedonia appears in a dream and says: 'Come over and help us.' The European mission can begin because Paul is prepared to be disciplined by boundaries which the Spirit sets. These prevent him, for one thing, from doing good, from evangelising – something which did not come into his particular remit at that time. Spirit-imposed boundaries kept Paul and his companions on course for the work entrusted. Such obedience enriched the church's unity in mission. It did not put it in jeopardy.

b) *Aphorizo* is used in Galatians 2:11–16 in quite a different sense. At the Council of Jerusalem (Acts 15), Peter, spurred by his contact with Cornelius, had argued strongly in favour of receiving Gentiles into the church without requiring them to observe certain prescriptions of the Mosaic Law, such as circumcision. In Antioch he had been sharing meals with Gentiles. For this he came under pressure from the party which insisted that Christians be circumcised. He then went back on his word and ate separately. This influenced even Barnabas to do the same. Paul takes Peter to task, accusing him of 'hypocrisy' – the word used by Jesus to condemn the outward show of religion of Scribes and Pharisees which contrasted with their actual conduct. Boundaries which split the faith-community, making fish of one kind of Christian and flesh of another, Paul insists, undermine the credibility of the gospel.

In the New Testament the world is spoken about in these two ways, which preserve or fracture unity. There is the world God loves and seeks to redeem, of which Christians are to be a serving and suffering component. On the other hand, there is the world which 'lies in the Evil One', which organises itself in hostility to God's will and way. This type of world Christians must reject. The example of Jesus is decisive. He accepted the terms of life which were available for all other people. His prayer to the Father was that his disciples should not be taken out of the world but that, there, they should be kept from the grip of evil (John 17:15). He came proclaiming God's Kingdom: the life of the world as we encounter it being transformed to work in the way God had in mind for it.

The relationship of church and world goes two ways. The church is called to make known to the world God's good will for it. But God works also outside the community of faith. Of the centurion who had pleaded for his servant's healing (Matthew 8) Jesus said: 'Truly I tell you, not even in Israel have I found such faith. I tell you many will come from the east and west and will eat with Abraham and Isaac and Jacob in the Kingdom of heaven, while the heirs of the Kingdom will be thrust into outer darkness.'

Take the case of Fidel Castro, reputed to be an atheist heading a Marxist state – which long ago became a 'lay society' (in the Latin American use of the word 'lay': not attached to any particular religious or ideological stance).

In 1973 I was with the newly founded Christians for Socialism in Chile. Fidel had been with them till a day or two before I arrived. After hours of listening and arguing with them he had said: 'With Christians such as you are, we who are Marxists can have not only tactical but strategic alliances.' In 1980, when I was in Nicaragua during the first anniversary of the revolution celebrations, I heard Castro, in the great square of Managua, urging the crowd not to take the Cuban Revolution for a model – rather to find their own *Nicaraguan* way of reconstructing society so that there would be justice for all. On two occasions in the early 1990s he invited leaders of Protestant churches to meet and converse with him for two days about faith and life. Every part of the debate was beamed out by radio and TV to the Cuban people. Thereafter Cuba departed from its Marxist foundation to become a society in which different religious bodies were free to make their way according to their ability to carry conviction. The last time I worshipped in a local church in Matanzas I found that my young neighbour in the same pew was a 'Communist Christian'. The noun indicated his basic conviction and commitment. The adjective emphasised a justice edge.

His experience chimed with Castro's own. The readiness of church authorities to collaborate with oppressive dictatorships had sickened Castro. He had turned to Marxism in a concern to establish justice. We should ask how he might have shaped out his life had he encountered church which had a clear justice commitment.[3]

In Scotland, John Calder, notable exponent of Samuel Beckett and all his works, author, dramatist, critic, agnostic, shared in discussions on the arts in Scottish Churches House consultations. At one point it was drawn to my attention that he always shared in services which I conducted. I had not noticed. So I got hold of him and said that we respected different positions held by participants – he need not feel obliged to take part in elements of the programme which he could not honestly affirm. He answered that he took part in the services because he wanted to. 'The concerns you express are concerns which I share. While you make them into prayers, I make them into meditations.'

In the human community, atheists can be a great resource: in posing deep questions about life's meaning, in exposing hypocrisy, in showing up the demonic nature of positions and attitudes which are ascribed to God's leading. In the human community, we may have separate convictions and callings but these should be held within a unity of respect for others and thoughtfulness before their particular understanding of what life offers.

Martin Luther, addressing the German nobility, said: 'The sphere of faith's work is worldly society and its order.' Dietrich Bonhoeffer affirmed the need for 'holy worldliness'.

Those who would be followers of Jesus Christ are called to live a holy life. The root of the word 'holy' implies separation. It is not separation *from* the world, but *for* God *in* the world.

WHAT GOD HAS JOINED ...

Life is all of a piece. A lack of faith may be shown not so much in words as in the way we get and use our money. The evangelical and the economic must go together. When members of the Iona Community hammered out a Rule in the 1940s, they found it important to include an economic discipline to keep members alert to the calling to get and use finance as a trust from God. This insight which applies on a domestic scale is also relevant on an international scale. In the Philippines, Senator Salonga (who was commissioned to try to trace the millions stashed away in secret bank accounts by the dictator Marcos) spoke to me about 'the *evangelical* necessity of research into the power of multinational corporations, lest the world get into a powerful grip which is other than God's'.

When, in the 1940s, I worked manually alongside basic labourers in industry, I found that the language of worship in church might have been the speech of alien invaders. When I took short services in break times for those who had to do maintenance work on machinery on Sundays, worship was real for them only when it met up with their own experience. I had to listen intently to their way of living and to their own way of putting things for worship to engage them. Worship and life must meet.

There are human beings who may be known as praying people, others as politically involved. Politics provides options for structuring society so that justice and equity may prevail. Praying that God's Kingdom may come implies confronting the evils and injustices in society and taking action to effect change. Praying people are called to be politically involved, the politically involved to be people of prayer.

Life is whole. What God has joined none of us must put asunder.

2.

MISPLACED BOUNDARIES

BOUNDARIES: DOGMA VERSUS ORTHODOXY

A shimmer of changing light

The beginning of the letter to the Hebrews makes it clear that, to live faithfully, we must relate vividly not to laws but to a life: 'Long ago God spoke to our ancestors in many and various ways by the prophets, but in these last days he has spoken to us by a Son.'

Those who are in controlling positions in churches at times get worried about the freedom this gives to all sorts of people to make what they can of Jesus Christ. They find it safer to freeze major features of his life into formulae to which they require assent. Dogma is belief become constipated, incapable of movement, needing an enema. It invites conformity. Orthodoxy invites on a journey.

Jesus made this clear. He said to his disciples: 'The one who believes in me will also do the works that I do.' At first sight this may seem to encourage attempts to freeze into dogmas Jesus' actions and words. But he goes on: '…and in fact will do greater works than these because I am going to the Father'. In his risen and ascended life Jesus calls his followers to larger insights and fresh ventures. Discipleship can never be static. Orthodoxy, true faith, cannot be formulated and imposed. It is dynamic, opening out fresh vistas, pressing us forward in ever-fresh ways. Systematic theology is not a construct of abstract propositions but a shimmer of changing light.

Wherever in any Christian tradition 'those who know' attempt to hold the whip hand over others, commitment to Jesus Christ may be replaced by a requirement of conformity to dogmas. 'For freedom Christ has set us free – don't submit to the old bondage,' says Paul (Galatians 5:1). Boundaries that separate off those who are in positions of authority from those who are expected to accept their line dutifully, split community. Had the principle of reception been adhered to faithfully in the Roman Catholic Church, it would have been recognised that married people must be free to use contraceptives.[4] Authorities have the right to test out doctrines. They then have to await the *church's* mind.

Orthodoxy takes seriously and together past tradition and present perceptions afforded by the Holy Spirit.

Jesus is the one final authority. The testimony to him in his life was that he *had* authority. All those who are set in positions of authority are to be tested according to whether they *have* authority. In 1 Corinthians 11:1, Paul asks his hearers to follow him *in the measure that* he follows Christ. This measure should be used to test all other types of authority. We have to be alert to identify those forms of separation which occur when a section of the church acts as if it were the 'real' church. If we hear 'The church says …', 'The church's position is …' we need to ask whether it is the church which speaks or ecclesiastics acting as if they were church.

The development of basic Christian communities in our time has led to reactions from the official church designed to test their orthodoxy. As I have known them all over the world, basic Christian communities provide, rather, a test of the orthodoxy of the official church. They find more in the life of Jesus than seems to get out in much worship and practice. Yet they do not reject the traditional church; they explore new ways for it to take. Throughout history, church has been rediscovered and reshaped in this fashion, inviting all to pilgrimage with the one who is the Way, Truth, Life. A succinct understanding of church held among basic Christian communities in Italy goes: 'The people of God must be self-convened before the Living-Word-in-Christ, without human masters.'

MISPLACED BOUNDARIES: INTERPRETING SCRIPTURE

Specialists in living

The interpretation of scripture is often taken to be a matter for academic specialists. Boundaries based on competence may be placed between them and ordinary members. But the members are also specialists in many forms of living which give competent access to scriptural truth. They are, moreover, Spirit-gifted. All kinds of knowledge need to be drawn upon to get to the heart of scriptural texts. It is in community, where different perceptions can support and challenge one another, that we get nearer to the truth.

On one occasion I was asked at short notice to prepare something on homelessness. I fastened on 'Foxes have holes and birds in the air have nests, but the Son of Man has nowhere to lay his head'. I consulted two commentaries and found that the scholar-authors were preoccupied with the phrase 'Son of Man': what did Jesus intend by using it here?, what did it convey to others in his time?, why did he not just say 'I have nowhere …'?, etc. It was clear that the scholars needed another specialist, a rough sleeper or migrant, to get them to the theological heart of the saying. Those who have instruments of scholarship to enable them to interpret scripture and those whose experience provides effective means to do so need one another.

There are some who simply reject the need for scholarship and scholars. For them the bible speaks 'directly to the heart'. They take it literally. They may say they believe in the bible from cover to cover. If so, they deceive themselves. We cannot take together both the psalmist's verdict that the way to treat enemies is to get hold of their little ones and dash them against a rock (Psalm 137:8,9) and Jesus' command to love enemies and do good to them.

On the road to Emmaus Jesus helped two disciples who knew by heart their scriptures (the Old Testament) to discern 'the things concerning himself'. It is clear that they had to sort these out from other things which were not to his mind. That is also our responsibility.

In 1984, a group from Britain established relationships with Italian basic ecclesial communities from Milan in the north to Naples in the south. There we came across three Roman Catholic communities that had taken journeys in seeking to understand the scriptures. These journeys had distinctive features (due to differences in members' situations and characters) and yet had a common thread running through their experience.

The Council of Trent (1545-63) had forbidden ordinary members to have access to the scriptures other than by official licence. Vatican II Council (1962-65) changed all that. The starting point of these three basic Christian communities could be stated thus: 'We were brought up to believe that this is the priest's book to be interpreted his way. Now we find it put in the hands of the whole church. We do not need a priest.' So they set to working directly on scriptural texts.

After some time they said: 'This is the wrong approach. The bible was written in different ways at different times. We are treating it as if we could get to the heart of it today without taking account of that.' So they looked out different commentaries and divided them among the members to get better understanding.

Again after some time they said: 'We are not there yet. We are no longer sitting at the feet of a priest. But we are sitting at the feet of commentators! There is a job still to be done to figure out what *we* make of the biblical texts so that we are helped to work out the way we should live in our time.'

At this point they sought out a non-dominating male or female scholar who was prepared to be attached to each group, who would listen and learn as well as contribute. Failing this, they looked for such a person who could be with them once a month. Insights of scholarship met up with insights drawn from experience.

In our day the scriptures are being opened out 'from below'. A Latin American peasant put a text in context regarding the Mosaic Law which forbade the eating of pork. He said: 'Pork was very prone to infection is those days. People did not know how to deal with that problem. We can now do so. So the scriptural word for us is that we are free to eat pork.'

Look at two concerns in our time which set boundaries between different members of the church: apostolic succession and homosexuality.

a) After the death of Judas, Peter stated the double requirement for a valid replacement to make up the Twelve: a man who had been with Jesus from the start of his earthly ministry and had met him in his risen life. That group died out and had no successors.

God does not seem to give a toss for immaculate succession. John the Baptist affirmed that from stones God could 'raise up children to Abraham' – note: not only children but children in the promised line. God is free to call anyone to any service. Look at the genealogy in St Matthew's gospel. The concern is not to be historically correct but to show how God was preparing for the coming of Jesus all through history. Women are included in the list – and such women! Tamar played the harlot to entrap Judah; Rahab was a prostitute and, with Ruth, was a non-Jew; Bathsheba was included through an act of adultery. The message is: God chooses whom God chooses and that is that.

The validity of a church depends on a succession of ordained males? To believe that is to fly in the face of scripture. Yes, the Twelve were all male. They were also Jewish and included some who were married. If the pattern of the Twelve is to be replicated, then those who are non-Jews and belong to a celibate group need not apply![5]

b) The condemnation of homosexuality is also supposed to be drawn from scripture. Ecclesiastically, it may be called 'a disorderly state', as if it were deliberately chosen to flout the sensitivities of society. This charge cannot stand. It has now been established that the tendency towards homosexuality can be recognised in the womb.

On what scriptural basis is the hostility founded?

Reference is made to the condemnation in the Mosaic Law. But there we find many more injunctions which should be taken as seriously – from detailed regulations for the purification of mothers after childbirth to the requirement that mixed fibres be not used in cloth-making (so much for shirts and blouses which are partly cotton, partly 'man-made' fibres). Why pick and choose which commands to obey? Moreover, is Jesus not to be heeded when he says: 'You have heard it said by old-timers … but I say to you …' (Matthew 5).

Recourse may then be made to Romans 1:26, 27. But note the word Paul uses. He is judging on the basis of his understanding of what is natural and unnatural. Now look at 1 Corinthians 11:13,14. He says it is natural for women to have long hair and men to have short hair. Tell that to some professional footballers! My mother thought it unnatural for women to wear trousers – the Chinese may not have seen eye to eye with her. The fact is that what is considered natural and unnatural varies in different cultures, in different ages, with different generations.

People of all sexual orientations should be welcome in an inclusive community where all are baptised into one body – Jews and Gentiles, women and men, slave and free.

In our time we are blessed that 'many prophets and righteous people longed to see what you see but did not see it, and to hear what you hear and did not hear it'. The bible is now in the hands of those who did not realise it was addressed to them directly.

In Bagakay, in the Philippines, I was with an exploited farming and fishing community. They did the work, others creamed off the profits. They thought that the bible was for rich people in towns. Then, unusually, a boy was given a chance to get school education. The scriptures came into the curriculum. He would return to the village, gather the people around, read a text and explain it. They found that the bible was their book! It was about farming and fishing, cooking and baking, eating and celebrating, facing setbacks such as a lost coin or a lost son.

One day the boy read a text and explained it. The villagers said that that was not the true interpretation. He said it must be – it was how his teacher explained it. That may be, they said, but that was not what the scripture actually meant. At that point they claimed the bible as the Word of God for them, made plain by the Holy Spirit. Inspired by it they started to fight the injustices they suffered.

To separate off a section of the church membership from others, as if there are some whose training give them true and exclusive access to scriptural truth, is to dishonour the gifts for perception of gospel insights distributed among the people. It is in community that scriptures are made plain. That calls for specialists in living as well as in scholarship.

MISPLACED BOUNDARIES IN THEOLOGICAL PERCEPTION

A shy African woman

Abstruse language has been a barrier. Jesus' theology given in parables dealt with challenges in familiar situations. His language made the parables accessible to the uneducated and the highly educated alike, so that none could escape facing decisions concerning true ways to live.

Different faiths have their own theologies.

Theology is a resource for all humanity. The concern to find what life is for is widespread. Thoughtful perceptions may come from seemingly unlikely quarters. Jesus said that we need 'ears to hear'. We need to learn to distinguish theological depth in ordinary situations and in ordinary speech. Take, as instances, questions concerning the authority of scripture and the reality of forgiveness:

A shy African woman always had recourse to the bible when faced with difficult situations. A neighbour mocked this habit. The woman was tongue-tied, could make no answer. On one occasion, in front of other neighbours, she was taken to task. 'There are so many books in the world – why do you always turn to one, just one?' At last words came. 'Other books I read – this book reads me.'

How many commissions on the authority of the bible have got further?

When Margaret and I served in Rosyth Parish Church an elder who worked as a lawyer was jailed for embezzlement. When he got out he found it very difficult to rejoin the congregation, some of whom had suffered financial loss at his hands. He would try – and then duck out at the last minute. At last he made himself share in the morning worship. I saw him afterwards and asked how it had been. Tears came to his eyes: 'They didn't either look down on me or fuss over me. It was just "Aye, Jim, glad you're back".' These were the words of a body which had become theologically mature. If people had used traditional words: 'Jim, we forgive you', that would have left them on the judgment seat, him on the sinner's stool. Their bringing him alongside made real the welcome back into their company.

Words themselves may prove at times to be inadequate vehicles for expressing theological insights. When, last century, the Church of Scotland owned the Gateway Theatre in Edinburgh, its director, George Candlish, concluded that the only way to give exposition to the book of Revelation was by ballet. In the Department of Mission in Selly Oak Colleges, students were free to present their work in whatever form proved appropriate. Two students presented a theological critique of Marxism in song and dance. Soloman Raj, who in India had trained girls to sing and dance the gospel, served at that time in the Communications department. He was able to provide a fully professional judgment on their offering.

In Panama, in 1980, members of a basic Christian community told me that they had gained a new appreciation of the significance of worship by using some of their own cultural resources:

Q. Do people build up the worship of the parish themselves?

A. The basic liturgy we have is the liturgy which the people prepare themselves in small groups. It is here that the relationship of concern is established, together with a desire to praise. The people deepen their understanding that when a prayer is made it is made to the Lord who is present, and the community must begin to look for ways to live it out. But the basic structure is rather classical.

The main liturgical contribution of the people came about very, very slowly – it was something indigenous. Some of the men in the community who played the guitar and drum, or the local folk instrument, the bocina, felt that the music they were singing in liturgical services wasn't really theirs. Their music was basically simple dance music, but music which called for creation and participation. So they began to choose folk melodies that came from their grandfathers and their great-grandfathers, and to pick out different sounds that would express basic ideas – penitence for instance.

In the indigenously produced Mass, the Misa Tipica, in 'Lord, have mercy', there is a kind of yodel called the 'saloma', which plaintively expresses the deep cry of need, of pain – the need for change and the pain that things don't change. The response to this cry is 'Glory to the Lord!'. The understanding of the people is that the cry of pain brings an immediate answer from the Lord who lives in pain, who is here in the midst of change. When one realises that the Lord is present with you in it all, you have immediate reason to rejoice.

Q. Do people dance in any of the liturgies?

A. Yes, on special occasions, at the offering of the gifts. What happens is that there is a moment in the liturgy where the people say, 'We want to give something; what is the thing that is most ours?' Well, it's dance. So a couple or a group will dance as a presentation, to make an offering. This happens for instance at the Feast of the Resurrection of the Lord. At Christmas, it is done in a sort of pageant. The people work out different reactions to the reality of the incarnation according to their own rural folk tradition. After the reading of the gospel there is a presentation of gifts to the Lord who is one with them again. It takes the form of a dance.

We had a marriage here at Pentecost. Pentecost is a great feast; it is actually the fiesta of the patron of our church. We didn't want to march around with statues of saints – it is hard to have the Holy Spirit incarnate in a piece of wax! But we had a wedding – a young couple who could dance very well. They decided to get married in rural costume, their real dress. They danced the offertory. It was beautiful, because it really expressed what they felt towards each other; and in their faces, in their way of dancing, you could see the desire to create together. The coming of the Spirit became vivid through their relationship, their relationship to the people, their offering of both to God.

Mention of the *saloma* ('which plaintively expresses the deep cry of need, of pain – the need for change and the pain that things don't change') reminds me of the strong emergence of the saxophone in the depression of the 1930s: 'When a lovely flame dies, smoke gets in your eyes'. I was in Iona Abbey one evening when a lone piper outside struck up the traditional Scottish song 'The Dark Island'. It made my mind fly immediately to the suffering servant in Isaiah 53. It gave the passage musical exposition.

In his poem 'As Kingfishers Catch Fire', Gerard Manley Hopkins speaks of the Christ 'who plays in ten thousand places, lovely in limbs and lovely in eyes not his'. The Greek word *charis*, used for the grace of Jesus Christ, is also used for comely movement in dance. The exuberance of Jill Halfpenny's jive on the TV programme *Strictly Come Dancing* surely reflects the realisation that we are made in the image of God and can pull out all the stops to celebrate our human existence.

I see a sign of the way in which we should use discipline as a means to freedom in the routines of Fred Astaire and Ginger Rogers. Such was Fred's exacting perfectionism in rehearsal that one dance, which ended at the top of a stairway, left Ginger with blood lining her shoes. The pair had a gift which went beyond accurate footwork. The discipline of training was crowned when they flowed into one another in the dance, in grace upon grace of movement. That is how it should be with the disciplines which enable people to grow into Christ. They are taxing, exacting. They prepare people for more than keeping in step with the Master. They anticipate a unity of life – as Jesus prayed to the Father: 'I in them and you in me that we may be completely one.' (John 17:23)

Sydney Carter put it:

> 'I'll live in you if you'll live in me,
> I am the Lord of the Dance,' said he.

The grace of Jesus Christ, 'lovely in limbs not his', may be found also in grimmer situations. In the sacrificial work of Médecins Sans Frontières, do we not see the Christ of TS Eliot?

> The wounded surgeon plies the steel
> That questions the distempered part;
> Beneath the bleeding hands we feel
> The sharp compassion of the healer's art
> Resolving the enigma of the fever chart. [6]

I do not say that people are *consciously* expressing faith in life-responses such as these. Was not Jill's jive a presentation to get the approval of judges, not God? I have no means of knowing, and they may well not know themselves. What I know is that in the parable of the last judgment those who are affirmed by Christ say, 'Where did you come in? Never saw you around!' They lived his way, that's all. It is enough to live his way.

When it comes to words, the great vehicle of communication is the bible, given exposition in sermons and even more effectively in hymns which gather insights down the centuries and have the great advantage of being sung communally.

THEOLOGY IN THE EVERYDAY

In a hunt for clothes

So often the concerns of theology seem to be directed to the high and low points of human existence. People have to face these from time to time and the relevance of theology may then become clearer to them. But what mainly preoccupies people's minds is life as it meets them daily. Jesus helped people to understand God's way with us by pictures from daily routines. There can be no greater theme than the coming of God's Kingdom. Jesus brought it home to his hearers by comparing it to yeast in baking, seed in sowing, light in darkness.

Do we not need to learn his gift for perception of God's way with us, illustrated by daily happenings? An aspect of Gethsemane was made clear to me in a hunt for clothes.

Margaret loved to have me accompany her when she wanted to freshen up an outfit. Say we were at the approach of winter and the general idea was to find a warm coat. When we had spare time we would go to likely stores, she to one part, I to another. We would take garments to one another with a 'How would this suit?'. In the end she might happily opt for a warm skirt and top. It mattered to her that I was accompanying her. It helped her to make her choice. But she might have come to the conclusion that, that year, coats lacked style, or were not the shade she wanted, or were too pricey. She had a range of options in mind to which I had no access: what garments might go over what or under what to freshen up an outfit for the winter. My part was to help clarify the decision.

Jesus Christ knew, by and large, the sacrificial life which the Father asked of him. But, restricted to the terms of human life, he had no access to the range of alternatives covering the Father's will for him. With the horror of crucifixion at hand, he wondered desperately whether he could escape and still do the Father's will. In the end, he accepted, with sweat like great drops of blood, the road to the cross – the Father's choice.

3.

CHURCH UNITY IN DIVERSITY

CHURCH UNITY IN DIVERSITY

'Every time you gather'

In Scotland, the Scottish Church Initiative for Union exercise proposed that some main features of churches as they are now be welded together into a common structure (inevitably producing an episcopal hierarchical framework, however modified). This might then be taken as a model! What impoverishment humanity would suffer if forms of church were tidied into one form! Imagine the loss if we did not have the Baptist tradition which not only keeps before us the need to think deeply about the way in which succeeding generations become members of the Christian community, but reminds us that we already have a basis for unity – though still to be adequately realised and expressed – in our baptism. The Salvation Army constantly presents us with a sign that Jesus Christ came especially for those with least prestige and power. The Society of Friends reminds us of the need to be an open and teachable community before God, seeking the guidance of the Holy Spirit, valuing that silence which makes us ready to listen when God speaks. And these are only three of the traditions which enrich church unity!

The major ecumenical challenge of our time, as far as the church is concerned, is for the churches to pool resources to equip the Christian community for an instructed and mature ministry in the world. In Britain, the loss of the Scottish Churches Open College[7] has been a setback. It helped people of different traditions to learn from one another while they learned from Jesus Christ through the Spirit what their calling should be. Those who thought that their service might be as clergy were given opportunity to test that out. Those who did not recognise such a calling might be taken by the scruff of the neck (as I was) and pointed in that direction. In this way the obstacle was overcome which made out clergy to be a special category of Christian; and equipment for ministry of all kinds was provided.

Why is it that, at times of financial stringency, it may be promising ventures that are cut off? As I write Scottish Churches House[8] has come under threat. Is anything more needed than the job description given to it from the beginning?:

To serve the world with integrity, especially using lay resources
To let the churches meet honestly and humbly about what separates them
To make fresh discoveries in the life of faith and devotion

In how many countries would Christians give their back teeth to get a common base for churches, as a house of hospitality and outreach, to fulfil such a mandate!

The New Testament witness is this: the equipping of the church for ministry in the world is not a top-down effort from 'those who know' to those who do not. It is a build-up effort to which every limb and organ in the body of Christ contributes. The church is furnished with gifts of the Spirit distributed among the membership. These need to be identified, valued and brought into play to build up the church and nourish its life in the world. A one-man band or one-woman band controlling what is meant to be a community exercise is out of place. Consider Paul's description of worship in 1 Corinthians 14:26–31. Those who call this an eccentric example are contradicted with the Greek word *hotan* at the start, '*every time* you gather'. He goes on to describe a fully participant development:

'Every time you meet for worship any of you can chip in with a hymn, some instruction, a revelation, an ecstatic word or its interpretation. Make sure the contributions are such as to build up the church … Of the prophets, two or three may speak while the rest weigh up what is said. If a revelation comes to someone nearby, the first speaker should give way. You can all in turn share insights, thus providing instruction and encouragement for the whole company.'

He does not seek to reduce the participation. He only asks that contributions be made in an orderly way, that they nourish the church's faith, and that members show courtesy to one another, giving way to fresh contributors. This is reaffirmed when he speaks of the Head: 'Jesus Christ … from whom the whole body, joined and knitted together by every ligament with which it is equipped, as each part is working properly, promotes the body's growth in building itself up in love.'

When Paul speaks of the meeting of such Christian communities he is referring to house churches. Not till the third century were separate buildings brought into use. In the small companies which met in houses, it would be easier for enquirers, the shy, the diffident gradually to gain confidence to participate in prayer and testimony. Basic Christian communities provide this kind of encouraging and enabling service all over the world today. In *Small Christian Communities Today* (Orbis, 2005) Cardinal Cormac Murphy-O'Connor testifies to the dynamic effects of encouraging into existence such small companies of seekers and finders. In his foreword, he says of his second parish:

'I helped to form ten of these basic communities and, before long, out of a parish of a thousand or so practising Catholics, about two hundred people were meeting regularly. It was in these faith clusters or communities that a whole mix of people – married, unmarried, young and old – discovered a new and deeper experience of faith through prayer, scripture, community and service to others. Through these small communities the parish came alive.'

An early contemporary sign of the world development of these communities was found in the emergence of the Iona Community in 1938. Once it had hammered out a rule of life, it found (largely through the prophetic insight of its deputy leader, Ralph Morton) that work needed to be done in small family groups as well as in plenaries. George MacLeod, the community's leader, saw in this development a 'John Baptist sign' in a world hoping for a 'new church'. As I write there are thirty-two such family groups in Britain with others in different parts of the world.

Making things new – the promise of the 'one seated on the throne' in Revelation 21 – requires new wineskins to cope with new wine, as Jesus observed. Even those who are disgruntled with the church-as-is find it hard to accept the disciplines which such change demands. It takes tough and persistent work to get members of congregations to develop and use their gifts so that they become effective limbs and organs in the body of Christ. I give a brief account of the work in Rosyth later on. It took two years' persistence to persuade members of the kirk session there to begin to equip themselves biblically; but then they got so excited by the relevance of the biblical texts to life in the home and in the dockyard that the problem became one of restricting them to an hour's bible study to start each meeting, so that some business might also be dealt with!

Small communities can do a great job in helping people to grow in faith. But even as things are, more can be done.

During Catherine Hepburn's memorable ministry in Gargunnock, she asked me on one occasion to stand in for her when she had to be elsewhere. I asked what the theme of the service was to be. She said 'bringing up young children in knowledge of the faith so that they were yet freed to think for themselves'. Now I must have been about eighty years old at the time – some distance from the realities! So I got hold of four parents and asked them if they would take the prayers. Oh no, they were too shy to speak in church. Then would they meet with me for an hour? No problem! I asked them to say what influences they would hope to be beneficial. In turn we looked at their own relationships with their children, those with the extended family, neighbours, teachers, schoolmates. They became animated. This was their territory. Every now and again I would stop and say, 'These are your words drawn from your own experiences – please write them down.' By the end of the hour we had prayers of confession, thanksgiving, intercession, self-offering, adoration, coming from the experience of those who knew what they were talking about. Since these were their thoughts in their words they were now quite ready to offer prayers in the service. (The only drawback was my failure to provide a microphone.)

Why on earth should a one-man band or one-woman band, poorly equipped for some of the worship, leave on the sidelines those who are well equipped to make it rich and real? Why on earth do those dumbed down in pews allow such a state to continue?

CHURCH-IN-THE-BECOMING

'The way that the Boss did it'

The present pope, when he was Cardinal Ratzinger, ventured to say that many churches other than Roman Catholic 'are not churches in the proper sense' (*Dominus Jesus*, para 17, published 6th August, 2000). This saying usurps the place of Jesus Christ who alone has the right to identify who are his. In any case, the claim can be discounted: a) in the parable of the last judgment the decision of who are Christ's true people is a turn-up for the books; b) the Cardinal took the matter of paedophile priests into his domain and then dropped it out of sight like a hot cake. Leaving abused children to continue to suffer is hardly the mark of a church 'in the proper sense'.

It is difficult 'from above' to discern a church which is always in-the-becoming. The church is 'born from below' – 'as each part is working properly … building itself up in love'. (Ephesians 4:16)

Tertullian, the Roman convert, writing somewhere around 200 AD, gave this picture: 'The churches, although they are so many and so great, comprise one primitive church founded by the apostles from which they all spring. In this way they are all primitive and all are apostolic' (*De Praescriptione Haereticorum*. 20). Professor PT Forsyth spoke of differently shaped 'outcrops of one Rock'. 'Reconciled diversity', which is now being used in ecumenical conversations, is a good phrase.

Christians who would grow up into the stature and fullness of Jesus Christ must surrender one-upmanship claims which are really power bids. One of the power problems of the Roman Catholic Church is its centreing so much on Rome – what Cardinal Konig called 'inflated centralism'. In its early life the church recognised four centres of orthodoxy: Jerusalem, Antioch, Alexandria, Rome. (Today Iona might be added.) Scots/Irish monasteries gave the primacy to Jerusalem.

How might we recognise church-in-the-becoming?

Professor Kenneth Latourette compared the historical phases of church life to incoming tides. At times there is a great move forward. There is a pause and the momentum seems to be lost. Then there is withdrawal. But that simply precedes a further move forward, a greater reach of the tide up the shore. I have experienced something like this in my own life. In the Church of Scotland in the 1960s, Kirk Weeks, the Tell Scotland movement and Scottish Churches House provided means for equipping lay people for effective ministries in the world. Then came the setback of the Billy Graham campaign. People who had been learning to draw on gospel resources to tackle situations they faced wherever they were, were asked to attend to wherever Billy Graham happened to be in his thinking. Mass gathering techniques persuaded people to flock to meetings. But 'the centre' did not hold. Once they got things into perspective, people realised that they were no better equipped to face life. The 'old style religion' approach with traditional hymns gave the Christian faith itself an outdated look for upcoming generations. The tide went right out.

It is difficult at times to discern whether a tide is going out or coming in. Many think the tide is going out. I believe it is coming in. Let me give just a few pointers:

❀ The Church Without Walls movement is providing new dynamism. Its objective picks up from Kirk Weeks, the Tell Scotland movement and Scottish Churches House thus: ' … to build a church shaped by friendship, shaped by the locality in which we find ourselves, shaped by the gifts of the people of God'. Features include a shift of mental attitude:

From a church focus to a Christ focus, following Jesus to see what church forms around him.

From settled church to church as a movement. Meeting people where they are.

From top-down church to upside down church, putting the local church at the centre of the agenda.

From faith as security to faith as risk, looking for new courage to break out of old routines.

❧ The Mungo Foundation exists to resource and empower the poor and excluded so that they have the dignity of children of God. Projects and services initiated and maintained in the Archdiocese of Glasgow are ecumenical in both senses. They are directed to the needs of the world. Those who serve come from different church traditions.[9]

❧ The Iona Community is a great beacon of light.[10]

❧ Canonmills Baptist Church in Edinburgh orders its life without an assigned ordained ministry. From time to time friends who are ordained are invited to take services. Otherwise worship, nourishment in the faith, different forms of service are provided for by the ministry of the whole congregation.

❧ The Scottish Episcopal Church Provincial Conference was given space in the October 2004 edition of *Open House*, the independent Scottish Roman Catholic magazine. Stephen Smyth reported. In character the conference was 'process and group-based' rather than 'expert-led'. Archbishop of Canterbury Rowan Williams challenged participants to 'find the gifts we have and the many unconsidered gifts which surround us'. John Miller, a parish minister and a former Moderator of the General Assembly of the Church of Scotland, asked that fresh attention be given to those gifts which are treated as 'stony ground'. He also asked that the church 'become involved in partnership with the crowd'.

❧ In the same edition of *Open House*, the chairperson of Catholics for a Changing Church put his finger on concerns which are widely shared in the church catholic. They included the following marks which, it was believed, should be characteristic of future church:

Ministries will be distributed strictly according to the ability, experience and competence of the candidates. No longer will an ordained man or woman be assumed to have the competences of an accountant, an employer, a social worker, a preacher, a manager and a committee chairman.

Ministers will not be required to live in presbyteries, separate from the people they serve, but new-style, mixed, residential communities will be formed as needed.

Clericalism will be dismantled, involving the abolition of distinctive dress for the ordained, and the abolition of higher status and of an idiosyncratic lifestyle which separates them from those they serve.

Ministries will be either full- or part-time, paid or unpaid, permanent or temporary, irrespective of whether a minister is ordained by a bishop or simply appointed and commissioned.

There will be new forms of education and training for ministry, where candidates are not cloistered away from those they hope to serve.

The contribution ends with this reflection on the repositioning of the ordained: 'They would no longer see themselves as clerics enjoying jurisdiction without accountability to those they serve, but as members of a team of servants with collective responsibility.' These insights, which pertain to the understanding of Vatican II, were recently reaffirmed in *The Tablet*: 'There is only one priesthood, the Priesthood of Christ, shared with the whole church, ordained and lay.'[11] Here we find common ground for many Christians.

A promising sign exists wherever privileged people move into deprived areas not only to serve but to live. In Lima, Peru, I encountered a group of young Christians who had trained to be teachers. The training could have provided them with upward mobility, financially and socially. Instead they went to live in a poor area of Lima, about half of them teaching to get income for all to live on, the whole group making itself available for whatever was needed to sustain and enlarge the life of the people. One place in Britain where a similar action is being taken is at The Eden Project in the Openshaw area of Manchester. There are nine Eden projects established in run-down parts of Manchester; these are fuelled on faith and the determination to make true what is found in Isaiah 62: 'No longer will they call you deserted or name your land desolate …' Gary Bishop, who runs the Eden Project, declares: 'Our work is incarnational – that's the way The Boss did it.'[12]

'But the time would fail me …'! I have not even mentioned developments with a heavy Christian investment which are in no way church-attached, such as the Scotland-based Centre for Human Ecology – surely a Kingdom of God enterprise, without that description being adopted.[13]

SO: WHAT CHURCH STRUCTURES WILL SERVE?

The trick is to bash institutions around and stick flowers in them

Let me now attempt to put things into broader perspective.

Movement and institution need one another. Without movement, institutions develop hardened arteries. Deprived of institutionalising, movements run into the sand. Moreover:

a) In our relationships with God, adequacy on our part is not on the cards. Our inadequacies do not hold God back. What is on the cards is humble offering of inadequacies. A few loaves and fishes, once trusted to Jesus Christ's hands, fed a multitude.

b) Human beings can outsmart dominating structures, dodge through gates before they close, knock institutions themselves into human shape. I loved what conductresses did with rigid official hats when they replaced male conductors in wartime. They bashed them around, stuck flowers in them, gave them a jaunty air. The trick is to bash institutions around and stick flowers in them.

c) Oppressive control by clergy and allies is not the monopoly of one type of church. In my own tradition 'the fear of Hell' has been brandished like a 'hangman's whip' to hold wretches in order.[14] Nor is prelacy confined to prelates. I congratulated a Church of Scotland parish minister, who was taking on a new charge, on a group of laity in the congregation who had enlarged their vision and developed their spiritual gifts through engagements at Scottish Churches House. He replied grimly, 'We'll let that fly stick to the wall!' Once he was installed he killed off what had been a promising lay development. He did not want competition. He considered it a threat to his own position. That local pastors should have such unregulated power is frightening.

d) There is that in the Christian faith, redolent of life and hope, which keeps bursting out in imperfect situations, persons and structures.

4.

NOW CONSIDER:
HIERARCHY, ORDINATION,
THE MINISTRY OF OVERSIGHT

CONSIDER: HIERARCHY

Hierarchy was a late and dodgy invention. It evidences a strong tendency to disinherit the church and concentrate on those of us who are clergy as if we were real church.

Hierarchy is late (Ignatius and Polycarp)

Over decades following Pentecost, hierarchical church structures are nowhere to be found. Care of the churches is entrusted to a team of people variously called elders/bishops/presbyters. Not till the beginning of the second century do we find a definite proposal to establish a hierarchical framework. In seven letters to churches, Ignatius of Antioch urged the extraction of one of the team to be called a bishop. He was to be made a focal point.

The proposal must have seemed weird because Ignatius had to pull out all the stops to try to persuade others.

He may have had a point at the time.

For one thing, the church must always be prepared to reshape its life to cope with changing circumstances throughout history. The value of the Czech clandestine church's experience for all churches today comes from the fact that it was prepared to change in quite a radical way to live the faith in an altered situation. For another, Ignatius and his contemporaries had a particular challenge to deal with. Prophets wandered round churches giving instruction and linking communities. In the first phase of the church's life, they held a place of special respect and played a leading role. But the church needed regular nourishment and building up which these wanderers could not supply. Moreover, the position could be abused. One character, Peregrine, was notorious for the way he traded on Christian hospitality. By the end of the first century one begins to find in the records respectful regard for prophets mixed with warnings about fraudulent operators. There is a search for more consistent provision for the upbuilding of the church.

This is clear from the *Didache* (*Teaching of the Twelve Apostles*), a very difficult text to date accurately; it could be from somewhere towards the end of the first century, or well into the second. Caution is mixed with commendation in the following advice:

'XI ... when the apostle departeth, let him take nothing except bread enough until he lodge again; but if he ask money, he is a false prophet. And every prophet who speaketh in the spirit, you shall not try nor judge; for every sin shall be forgiven, but this sin shall not be forgiven. But not everyone that speaketh in the spirit is a prophet, but only if he have the ways of the Lord. So from their ways shall the false prophet and the prophet be known. And no prophet who orders a meal in the spirit eateth from it, unless indeed he is a false prophet; and every prophet who teaches the truth, if he do not that which he teaches, is a false prophet ... Whoever, in the spirit, says, Give me money or something else, you shall not hear him; but if for others in need he bids you give, let no one judge him ...[15]

XIII ... But every true prophet who will settle among you is worthy of his support.

It could well be that Ignatius saw the need for a firmer church structure to allow the membership to be nourished and built up in the faith in a regular manner rather than being at the mercy of wandering prophets. Yet there were inherent dangers.

Polycarp simply ignores Ignatius' proposal. Though in his letter to the Philippians there is not much reference to church structures, he sticks with the communal model of care, making no mention of the extracted bishop, e.g. (section VI) 'let the elders be compassionate towards all'. Was he wary of some of Ignatius' ways of putting things? In Ignatius' letter to the Ephesians (section VI) he writes: 'It is evident, therefore, that we ought to look upon the bishop even as we would do upon the Lord Himself'! In his letter to the Trallians II.I, he says, 'be subject to the bishop as to Jesus Christ'; and in the missive to the Smyrnaeans VIII.1, 2, where Polycarp was bishop, he goes the length of asserting 'whatever he [the bishop] approves is also pleasing to God'!

Did Polycarp see the shadow of a prince-bishop looming ahead? Yet Ignatius also writes, in his letter Trallians (section III), 'let all reverence deacons as Jesus Christ'. It seems to me that Ignatius simply pleads for appointed officials to be more in charge – hierarchy at this stage is hardly a pyramid of power. He advocates the bishop's presiding at the Eucharist (after all, he was the equivalent of a parish minister today) but does not insist that, in his absence, another ordained person preside, as became the practice much later: only that the bishop approve whoever takes his place. Indeed, in the end, he does not consider a bishop essential to the life of the church. On his way to martyrdom he writes to the Romans (section IX): 'Remember in your prayers the church of Syria, which now enjoys God for its shepherd instead of me: let Jesus Christ only take care of it, and your charity.'

Note that in the same century it continues to be affirmed that the priesthood on earth which accompanies Jesus Christ's High Priesthood is that of the whole church. Thus Irenaeus in AD 167 wrote 'all righteous men hold the priestly order' (*Adversus Haeresis* IV.20); Tertullian in AD 192 declared 'are not all the laity priests? It is written "he has made us a Kingdom and priests to God"' (*De Exhortatione Castitatis* VII). Later, in AD 400, Augustine wrote 'as we all are Christians on account of our mystical charism, so also all are priests since they are all members of the One Priest concerning whom the Apostle Peter says "a holy people, a royal priesthood"' (*City of God* XX.10).

At this stage of history there is not a form of hierarchy developed in power-layers. Ignatius is still a team player. For all his elitist concept of the extracted bishop (as if by mere appointment bishops became mirrors of Jesus Christ) he sees bishops and deacons to be intimately related to the communities in which they serve. It is the company of presbyters whom he considers to be trustees of the apostolic faith, not a succession of bishops extracted from that company. But his prising out of individuals had a strange result. He pled that the bishop be given respect and love. Fair enough. But the secular urge to translate this into higher and lower ranking in time proved too strong. It even came to the point where some claimed that the validity of churches depended on an unbroken succession of these individuals.

Consider what a weird idea this is. It is as if there were a Kingdom of God league table. Placings on it are determined not by the performance of the teams but by the lineage of the team coaches! Who would think of such a concept other than the coaches' own trade union?

Hierarchy is dodgy (Columbanus and Pope Boniface IV)

Only too readily hierarchy lends itself to top-down power on the one side and to deference and compliance on the other. Is it not peculiarly difficult to exercise power in a servant way in a hierarchical structure? There are clearly people who hold high office in the church who are humble in life and relationships. But is it possible for a hierarchy itself to have a humble, enabling form – especially if layers of power remove decision-making further and further from the realities of daily life in which faith has to be implemented? Pressure to conform in a hierarchical structure and resistance to the pressure can be illustrated from history.

The difference in style between Rome-based and Irish/Scots monastic communities in the six and seventh centuries provides pointers for our time. Rome-based orders were deferential, polite. They considered the Irish/Scots to be crude and insensitive, quite lacking in the finer diplomatic arts. A letter to Pope Boniface IV from Columbanus, a contemporary of Columba, might be described as 'courteous' rather than 'polite' (Since the time of Chaucer, courtesy, with its combination of respect and honest speech, has been presented as the genuine offspring of truthful dealings, while politeness is its smooth-spoken bastard.)

The start of the letter is not so much one of deference as of obsequiousness: 'To the most illustrious head of all the churches of the whole of Europe, that specially gentle pope, that eminent prelate, Shepherd of shepherds, that most revered watcher: to a most dignified one the most humble presumes to write: the least to the greatest; a rustic to a denizen of the city; a man tongue-tied to one who is most eloquent; the last to the first ... ' [16](Is this an exercise in grovelling? Or a softening up for what follows?) He urges the pope: 'If personalities trouble you think not of the man who speaks but of what he says. For better are the wounds dealt by a friend than the hypocritical embraces of an enemy'; and he later makes it clear that it is love for the papacy that motivates him: 'Do not despise this little piece of advice given by a foreigner, for you have taught him and it is your cause that he is championing.' In such a context, he questions the pope's orthodoxy: 'I confess to you that I am grieved at the ill repute of the chair of Peter'; and he stoutly affirms the orthodoxy of the Irish church as providing his basis – 'the catholic faith as it was first delivered to us from you, the successors, that is, of the holy apostles, is retained among us unchanged' – and challenges him to be alert: 'Your vigilance will be the salvation of many as, on the other hand, your carelessness will bring many to ruin.' He chides the pope: 'Lest I seem to flatter you even more than is right, it is also to be deplored that you did not, as you should have done long ago, take the first steps in zeal for the truth, seeing that you have the lawful authority', for 'it is a matter of grief and to be deplored if the catholic faith be not held in the Apostolic See'.

The problem? Reports circulated that the pope was consorting with heretics and was imbibing their teaching. Hence: 'I urge you, my fathers and my own superiors, to drive away confusion from the faces of your sons and disciples who are put to shame on your account; and what is more than this, that the mist of suspicion be removed from the chair of Peter. Call therefore together a council that you may clear yourselves of the charges brought against you.'

But suppose the council find the charges proven? That would allow the true situation to be tackled! 'Now it is your fault if you have strayed from loyalty and 'rendered vain your first faith'; rightly do your juniors resist you and rightly do they not communicate with you ... For if these things are true ... those who have always kept the orthodox faith, whosoever they may be, even if they seem your juniors, will also be your judges; for they are the orthodox and true Catholics since they have neither received nor defended any heretics or suspects, but remained zealous for the true faith.' With the innocence of a con man he adds 'pardon me if I have said anything that might offend pious ears ...'

In the letter Columbanus takes the line 'if these things are true' – and so stands open to correction. That does not prevent straight talking to someone who, when all is said and done, just has a job. The whole letter, though discursive at times, has contemporary significance.

The present pope, when Cardinal Ratzinger, in his book *The New People of God*, wrote: 'The church needs men with passion for the truth and prophetic denunciation. Christians ought to be critical even in regards to the pope himself, because certain panegyrics do great harm to the church and to him.'

Brazilian Bishop Pedro Casaldaliga, in a fraternal circular letter sent as we entered this new millennium, wrote: 'The reform of the papacy and its Curia would make possible – with the "autonomy" of the Spirit and the expectations of the universal church – many reforms in co-responsibility, collegiality, inculturation, legitimate pluralism, and in ministries.'

Should responses to Pope John Paul's challenge to assess Rome's claims in the encyclical *Ut Unum Sint* be marked by politeness or courtesy?[17]

To complete this picture: there is evidence that hierarchies can reject the pyramid-of-power structure and be made to work humanly.

Basic ecclesial communities in Mexico, the Philippines and Nicaragua

The genius of Bishop Mendez Arceo in Mexico was to found the whole diocese on basic ecclesial communities – small groups of 8 or 10 people who sought to live the faith in face of the challenges of their day and thus to 'grow up into Christ'. Community life was founded on Christ, nourished by bible and Eucharist, given to prayer, expressed in the world in struggles for justice and peace. Diocesan conferences drew directly on their experience for a critical assessment of the past life of the church and for forward planning.

The genius of Bishop Escaler in the Ipil diocese in Mindanao, the Philippines, was to turn a pyramidical structure into a spiral and press it down to become a spring. Four times a year it tightened from the 1,200 basic ecclesial communities who met weekly – through Sunday *capilya* services led by laity, through monthly *zonas* for leaders appointed by the grassroots, through parish and district gatherings – to a Prelature Assembly with 120 or so representatives nearly half of whom were women. It then rewound back to the small communities, bringing fresh vision and dynamic to the base. Here was hierarchy operating as a pulse of life.

On the spot I interviewed a medical missionary. She said:

'When I left, these people would be cowed and voiceless in any assembly of this kind. They would have accepted that it was their superiors who had the right to tell them what to do and think, and they would not have dared to raise a word in protest. But what have we here? Bishop Escaler is not even taking the chair – it is a young layman who guides the Assembly, with the bishop contributing from time to time with the others. Women with families, fishermen, landless labourers, young people are making thoughtful and articulate contributions. They listen carefully to others and take their own share in trying to discern the will of God for the diocese. And their sense of dignity before God, their confidence, their determination – all spring from their faith! Many times they are afraid as they experience the violence and destructiveness that they meet in daily experience. But they stand, and they stand together!'

The dynamic found in Ipil was also evident in services in Iglesia La Merced in Nicaragua. The priest worked with a hand-held microphone. When it came to prayers, members of the congregation shouted out what and who should be prayed for, or said: 'Gimme the mike' and offered the prayers themselves. When it came to the sermon the priest started off with four or five minutes reflection on the biblical passage for the day; then members of the congregation, one by one, built up the sermon. This was no shallow, off-the-top-of-the-head stuff. The congregation met during the week in seven basic ecclesial communities, considered who and what should be prayed for, and worked on the biblical passages for the Sunday. Members could make well-prepared contributions and be enriched by hearing those which came from the other six basic ecclesial communities. Growing up into Christ the Head – that was in evidence before my very eyes.

There always have been 'high ups' who are humble. Bishop Helder Camera replaced his throne with an ordinary chair. It was said of Pedro Casaldaliga that he was 'un obispo a medida del Evangelio' – a 'gospel-sort-of bishop'. What we need are humble structures as well as humble people. It is well to continue to remain wary of hierarchical forms when they put layers of power on top of one another so that decisions are made further and further from the people. In Mexico, Ipil, Managua, the living juices of faith worked out at the base found expression in policies across the whole diocese.

CONSIDER: ORDINATION

A shortage of clergy?

In the early church, forms of ministry were not fixed and immovable, nor did they imply full-time setting apart. The laying-on of hands might be for a long-term assignment, as with Timothy, or for a missionary journey whose length could not be predicted, as with Paul and his companions. People were set apart for as long as the job took. As situations changed, different gifts might be called for and be brought into play. For instance, those who exercised a prophetic ministry in one decade might be destined for teaching responsibilities in the next decade. The list set out in Ephesians 4:11,12 – apostles, prophets, evangelists, pastors, teachers – does not add up to a series of defined offices but to a series of roles (and church members were not stuck with one role all their lives). But, in time, there seems to have been some assimilation to secular thought and practice. The Greek word *taxis* is a word for deploying forces so as to engage an enemy effectively in battle. Its equivalent in Latin, *ordo*, from which come 'church orders' and 'ordination', has the same intention but has a more static flavour and developed, in time, more emphasis on rank and position. In secular society, *ordo* came to denote the privileged class over against the plebs, the 'common herd'. With such an idea of order extant in society, the idea of higher and lower grades of churchmanship came to infiltrate Christian thinking. (There was always a danger that the ordained would feel threatened and that this would happen. Those of us who are ordained live with this insecurity: there are no features of our ministry which are not features of the ministry of the whole people of God.) Ordained ministry must be seen to exist within the whole church for the strengthening of the whole church without the security of separate validation.

Some traditional understandings of ordination load the word with an ecclesiastical weight which it cannot bear. It is taken to convey an indelible character which separates the ordained from other baptised Christians. Modern translations of the bible rectify the matter. Where, in the Authorised Version, reference is made to the ordaining of disciples (Mark 3:14, John 15:16), the Greek is now simply translated as the word 'appoint' – that is all that is meant.

Arguments about the validity of orders fall flat when it is recognised that the substantive ministry is not that of the ordained but of the people of God. When Bishop Lesslie Newbigin and I moved to the Selly Oak Colleges we transferred our church membership from the Church of Scotland to the United Reformed Church. At a meeting in London the question was raised: In light of the shortage of ordinands should an auxiliary ministry be thought of? We came out with the same words: 'That is what our ministry is – auxiliary to the ministry of the whole church.'

There is a shortage of clergy? If those of us who are ordained are not committed to equipping the whole church to carry out its ministry in the world, there may still be too many of us.

CONSIDER: 'THE MINISTRY OF OVERSIGHT'

Celtic monks, and a church in the Chuloteca district of Honduras

In the old dispensation a sacrificing priesthood was inserted between God and the people. That was done away with in Jesus Christ, who is the only Mediator between God and humanity. But the longing for an intermediary agency has persisted. It has led to some kind of two-way communicating neck being inserted between Christ and the church. Agencies – hierarchical, bureaucratic, clergy-based, professional – have taken upon themselves or have been given responsibility to take oversight of others. If hierarchies and bureaucracies had learned the skill to be an empowering service, providing modest enabling resources, that would be a positive contribution (after all, good administration is important). But too often the role they adopt is in-between. Then the nature of church is distorted. We even find situations where the intermediate agency acts as if it were real church to which the membership should accommodate itself. How distant this is from Paul's description in Ephesians 4:15,16. He speaks of Jesus Christ as the Head and goes on: 'from him the whole body, joined and held together by every supporting ligament, grows and builds itself up in love as each part does its work'. The only genuine ministry of oversight is in fact a mutual ministry of all the members who care for one another and help one another to live faithfully. All kinds of people with all kinds of gifts of the Spirit are called to contribute to the upbuilding. Also, Paul's advice to 'appoint elders in every town' (Titus 1:5) was made known by his disciple associates, one of whom would have written the Titus epistle. A body of people, variously called elders/bishops/presbyters, was appointed to care for the good of local churches. Though it is likely that Peter was martyred in Rome, he was never Bishop of Rome. In his day there were no such things as individualised bishops. Care of the churches was a communal responsibility in Rome as elsewhere.

Moreover, throughout history, those who have a special gift to enable the ministry of a whole community have often been people without prestigious training – animators, delegates of the Word, catechists. These are not separated off to be equipped for the work. The delegates of the Word and the catechist whom I encountered in the Chuloteca district of Honduras gave up one weekend a month to be more adequately fitted and formed for the work. Over years this produced a richly resourced service. It also encouraged other people with gifts of the Spirit to exercise their many ministries.

Jesus is the Head, we are the body; He is the Shepherd, we are all sheep; He is the Vine, we are all branches; He is the Capstone, we are all building stones.

Part of the problem about any assumption of superior rank lies in the interpretation of the prefix 'epi', as in *episcopos*, the Greek word for bishop, and episcope. It has been taken to identify a person or an office which is over others – an overseer who gives oversight. But that is not the core meaning of 'epi'. The prefix indicates, in its essence, 'giving concentrated caring attention'. This implication is patent in the action of Czech bishops who had been jailed who, when they emerged, no longer took oversight of a diocese but turned full attention to the needs of the poor and the excluded. It is confirmed in James 1:27 where the expression of true religion is declared to be in concentrating on the needs of widows and orphans, deprived people in that society.

Since the Czech example which follows comes from the Roman Catholic tradition, my illustrations have mainly been drawn from that tradition. But in almost all religious societies (the Quaker certainly excepted) there has been a dependence on in-between forms. When Jesus Christ should have been looked to as the source of life, often some dogmatic formulae, to which assent is required, have replaced him as the final reference point. The wonder with which the epistle to the Hebrews starts – that whereas, in the past, at different times and ways God spoke through the words of prophets, he has now spoken in a life – then gets lost. The wonder and challenge we are faced with is to feed on that life and be confronted by it directly and continually – if need be in face of secular and ecclesiastical authorities alike. In my own background, which is catholic and Reformed, those of us who are clergy were also trained as if our role was to be intermediaries. What was given to us would allow us, in turn, to teach the faith to congregations and provide them with pastoral care. True, we worked in community with kirk sessions and presbyteries. That was an important feature. But we were given no equipping in awareness of and in techniques for identifying the gifts of the Spirit distributed among the people of God and for freeing members to exercise these in a variety of ministries. Those who felt they had a calling to emphasise preaching too often produced followers rather than enabling disciples to grow and mature – and expected people to come to them rather than go out to where the people were. Contrast this with bands of Celtic monks who brought to the surrounding area, with the gospel, skills in healing and building and farming. People were supposed to start with the minister's vantage point rather than their own!

In the separation of those of us who are clergy from the rest of the membership, there have been decisive moments. In the Edict of Milan, 313 AD, Constantine gave the Christian faith secular legitimacy and bishops assumed the purple of magistracy. In the sixteenth century, the Council of Trent decreed that there should be a seminary in every diocese for the training of priests in orthodoxies of the faith. This form of equipping became general in Western churches. The objective was to have a competent pastorate/priesthood. But the separating of ordinands resulted in their being made a special category to which distinctive power and status were accorded. Community was broken and the nature of ministry misrepresented. Jesus said: 'One is your Master, the Christ; you are all brothers and sisters.' This not only depicts his relationship to us; it gives a picture of the church as a horizontal community of believers.

5.

BREAKING RANKS TO RENEW COMMUNITY – A CZECH EXPERIENCE, AND A ROSYTH PARISH

THE CZECH CLANDESTINE CHURCH

The Czech Roman Catholic Church, where it formed small communities in the underground rather than collaborate with the Communist occupation, knew what it was to prune back the life of faith to its essentials. We can learn from that experience.

Jan Kofron is a recognised leader. He was trained and ordained clandestinely. At a gathering of basic ecclesial communities in Cochabamba, Bolivia he shared with others what the pruning entailed when a power was in charge which was hostile to the church's life in his country. (Extracts from his texts will kept in his own words, as was promised him, and the Prague underground Community will be given a capital 'C'.) The Cochabamba consultation took place in 1999 – it is of events up to that date that he speaks, which required 'an authentic living of the Christian message under new conditions'.

Jan Kofron sets the scene:

The persecution of the church was so strong during the Communist regime! The Church of Silence (Ecclesia Silenti – the initials E.S. are sometimes used)[18] has represented perhaps the most clandestine level of the church surviving under the Communist regime in Czechoslovakia …

The Community's origin had been a quite spontaneous one. The occupation of Czechoslovakia by the Soviet troops in 1968 brought again a new oppression of the church that, in comparison with the first Communist campaign of the '50s, was more sophisticated and less openly cruel. All ecclesiastical activity was under the control of the Communist authorities, which was why all clergymen were obliged to possess special permission for performing pastoral ministry. All those who were witnessing to the Christian message in an authentic way were practically considered to be enemies of the regime. The only activity that was permitted was liturgy in the churches. The worse it was, the better for the Party – for its aim was full liquidation of religious life in the country!

From a sociological point of view our Community was very diversified. There were basic workers as well as university students. Our only aim was an authentic living of the Christian message under new conditions. The Community came into existence step by step, quite spontaneously. There did not exist any project on how to set up such an informal unit of the church!

There was spiritual starvation at the very beginning. The main focuses were, accordingly:

Prayer
Liturgy
Koinonia – community – togetherness – sharing
Leaders formation (practically each member of the group was leading another group)

The Eucharist is the centre of community life. This is not a question of folk piety but of real rooting in Christ's self-offering. In another word, the spiritual life is life. Life in the Community draws its origin from the Sunday Eucharist. A mere activism – without spiritual underpinning or Christ-centred radicality – could be misleading in determining attitudes to such concerns as trade unionism, environmentalism, charitable activities, etc.

Common prayer was not considered as a sort of religious custom or duty but as an existential need. The conditions of persecution were enabling Community members to discern crucial points in their life. (From such a point of view the persecution was undoubtedly a gift.)

Since the time when several members of the Church of Silence were put in prison, the Community members, wherever they are, pray daily at 8:30 pm, their evening prayer. At the very beginning this was an expression of solidarity of the group with those imprisoned members. This has become a custom of the Community members and a duty for ordained members. At special occasions or troubles special prayer meetings are held.

Contact established

It was at a World Council of Churches conference in Brno in 1991 that I first made contact with members of small communities that had formed the Czech underground church during that Communist occupation. I had linked up with their Hungarian counterparts in 1987. The occupation there was in force at that time. One had to move very cautiously. Insensitive attempts to make contact could have exposed networks to penetration by the secret police. The consequences for members would have been jail sentences.

I had helped to interconnect the small church communities in Eastern Europe with those in the West. Sizable delegations of Hungarians and Czechs took part in the Seminar of Basic Christian Communities in Geneva in November/December 1995. To follow up that gathering, I was invited to share in the summer meeting of the Czech Community members in August 1996. It was instructive to spend almost a week with them.

For one thing, I discovered a church which had reshaped its life. It had got the better of harsh circumstances – and had used them to deepen its faith and to prune away inessentials in its practice. Here was promise of a future church which principalities and powers would never be able to subdue. For another thing, the affection shown for the Iona Community was surprising and heartwarming. The Iona Community seemed to have been installed in the affection of members as the earliest sign of fresh forms of Christian community marked by new, vibrant priorities. A decade before the Soviet troops took control of Eastern Europe and put pressure on churches either to collaborate or develop secret cells; two decades before there were stirrings in Latin America: Scotland provided a 'John Baptist sign' pointing towards church renewal. Czechs could see one Spirit at work in the development of new forms of community from that point forward. Their own history testified to the reality of their crucial place in that new pulse of the Spirit.

The building in which we met in 1996 had been purchased at a low price in the early 1980s. It had been owned by ecclesiastical authorities. The overt purpose in taking it over was to provide a centre for sporting activities. The local Communists congratulated the negotiator in acquiring, for a healthy purpose, premises which had previously been dedicated to 'outdated superstitious practices'. They did not know that they were speaking to a priest of the clandestine church!

At that time it had no windows, the walls had big holes in them, the roof was porous. In 1996 there was still no heating in the building so winter meetings were difficult. A pump in the yard was the only source of water, which had to be carried in in buckets for washing, cleaning and cooking. Outside toilets reminded me of those used in my early years by my crofter uncles! People crammed up happily in dormitories and small rooms. What might have been taken to be drawbacks provided occasion for mutual support and enrichment of the common life. One aspect of the gathering each summer is manual work in which all share to repair, renovate and extend the property – as we did on Iona in the early days of the Community. They found, as we did, that such work deepens community living.

In that company were two bishops, two priests, deacons, adult laity, adolescents and younger children. Their way of life stood in contrast with much which marked the traditional church. 'Persecution is not to be courted,' said one of the bishops to me, 'but if God gives gifts in such a time they are not to be discarded when times change. They must be weighed and, in new circumstances, be given appropriate expression.' One way in which his own life testified to such gifting was as follows: His role as a bishop had been detected. He had been jailed for six years. Gypsies shared the prison in which he was incarcerated. He took the opportunity to learn their language and establish trusting relationships with them. On his release he was able to be among them and to minister to them as would have been impossible had he never been jailed. He gave loving care to them and to ex-prisoners and other people excluded and devalued in society. These people were served by the provision of Emmaus houses of refuge and resource. That provision, not a diocese, now claimed him.

LIFE IN THE UNDERGROUND

Jan Kofron: *Communicating in the underground was very difficult. All phone calls were tapped and monitored. To use phones we had to develop a code. Numbers were given to particular families, to days and to times. You had to make some innocuous remark involving numbers to indicate where and when a meeting would take place. My own family were given the number 12: if I mentioned 12 apples in a conversation that would indicate that it was at our house that a meeting would take place. I have seen me forget a relevant number (we did not put them down on paper) and had to travel across Prague to check it out before putting the information in a coded message! ... we shared no more than was strictly needed for our survival ... we had to be alert for infiltration ... Secret meeting places at all hours of the day or night were required also for the training of those who would be called to officiate in the underground church. The communities selected candidates. Direct knowledge of the qualities of future leaders who had been hardened in the furnace of persecution offered good guidance. The training provided was much more thorough than that available to those ordinands who were willing to play ball with the Communist regime. For instance, Josef Zverina and Otto Madr, who had taught dogmatic theology and moral theology respectively, both spent about fourteen years in jail and continued their ministry there ... the persecution was actually not a disaster, but a new and very significant, eloquent salvific act of the Lord who promises not to leave his church.*

Fridolin Zahradnik, a bishop in the hidden church, jailed for six years under the Communists, gave me the context in which ecclesiastical authorities operated:

I.M.F: Could you tell me how and on what authority you were consecrated a bishop?

F.Z: A group of bishops of the hidden church decided that three more married priests should be consecrated as bishops – if possible, without drawing upon them the suspicions of the state police. I was one of the chosen. Our consecration was according to the forms of the Eastern tradition whose priests can be married, not the Roman tradition. It was all done legally. Jurisdiction was given. But it still had to be done secretly, out of sight of the secret police.

I.M.F: Did the police crack down hard on clergy?

F.Z: In 1950 all the bishops but two were arrested. The archbishop was put under guard and thereafter dispatched to Rome. Pope Pius XII then provided the same jurisdiction as had been previously provided for Mexico at the time of persecution. Normally Rome needs to know about the consecration of new bishops. In the Mexican and Czech situations, where Rome was out of contact, there could be consecrations without reference to Rome. Priests were also given the same kind of freedom (except that only bishops could ordain) to act without following normal procedures.

In 1949 the Vatican had consecrated four bishops to act secretly in Czechoslovakia but these were either soon arrested or remained inactive through fear. Yet one Jesuit who was consecrated went on to consecrate three more Jesuits so that four were again operating. This kept intact the succession which is officially recognised. In a case of need, one bishop, acting alone, was free to consecrate; but I was always able to have two other bishops with me when I presided at a consecration.

I.M.F: How does the official Vatican authority now regard the hidden church?

F.Z: It really counts it okay. When the pope visited he commended those who had kept the faith at sacrificial cost during the Communist occupation – who had suffered imprisonment, torture, death as a result. The problem is with the Czech hierarchy internally, some two-thirds of whom had been collaborating with the regime. Some bishops who were consecrated after the revolution still 'sat on two chairs'. The two-thirds were against the hidden church, largely because they had a bad conscience about collaborating.

I.M.F: Are groups which belonged to the hidden church still to be found all around the country?

F.Z: We are in a changed situation. Bishops and priests of the hidden church are found all around the country serving openly – but they still are in contact with all kinds of groups in the parishes which once had a secret life.

I.M.F: But are these groups now part of parish structures?

F.Z: They take responsibility for, and share in, developments in the parishes, but at the same time insist on getting the space needed for continuing in the life of their communities. They don't stay apart. They now attend public worship as a matter of course … Ordained people who had been operating clandestinely put in a normal week of work and at the *weekend are available in the parishes. There are four to five Masses on Sundays and three on Saturdays. There is a great shortage of priests, so all are needed.*

I.M.F: *Looking back, what would you say brought the hidden church into being?*

F.Z: *We discovered that a bad situation also brought gifts. Opportunities for pastoral care appeared, both inside and outside jails, such as had never been recognised previously. We tried to share these discoveries with traditional bishops but they did not want to listen; they found security in the familiar way of doing things. I and my colleagues refused to be tied to dioceses. We believe that we should concentrate on the poor, whom the traditionalists have neglected.*

'He just has a job': questions of leadership

On one occasion I began several questions with the words 'Bishop Jan' and was pulled up by my interpreter.

'He's just Jan, you know. If you add 'bishop' it sounds like a title. He doesn't have a title. He just has a job.'

A simple statement conveys profound theological insight! It can be put alongside Jesus' comment in Matthew 23:8: 'You have one Master, and you are all brothers and sisters', and Paul's in 1 Corinthians 12:25: 'there should be no division in the body but … its parts should have equal concern for each other'. In the body of Christ different parts have different jobs to do. What is important is that together they build up the body. When the parts fulfil different complementary functions each is then due only the servant status which Jesus Christ accorded.

Some years ago I was with an Indian congregation (they did not want to be called 'original native Americans') in Guatemala. I asked the priest this question: 'Who would be trusted to guide the community especially at crisis points?' He said that no one coming in as I did from the outside would be able to spot the man or woman they turned to. He or she would not be upfront, would play no significant part publicly, would have no high profile. But when the community wanted to get clear about the road ahead they would sit around that person and listen. They would know in their hearts that the advice given was sound.

To my knowledge, all proposals for uniting church structures in Britain have advocated one type of structure, a hierarchical one, however modified and democratised. This will inevitably happen when different features of churches as they are are welded together. It may mean that the drawbacks of pyramidical structures are not examined critically enough. Jesus spoke of the way in which princes of the Gentiles exercised power – and warned his followers that that must not be the way they take. Was it in an unguarded moment that Pope John Paul referred to a raft of new cardinals as 'princes of the church'?

'A nearly new phenomenon': The Czech experience

In a time of pruning, those who are concerned for the life of faith sometimes have recourse to abstract, theoretical ideas for reshaping church life. But there is tried and tested evidence to draw upon. Concretely, in our time, the church has been pared back to essentials.

Echoes of the early church are found in the pruning back which those Czech Christians who refused to collaborate with the Communist regime found necessary for survival in the underground. One basic change reminds us of Paul's description of a gathering of Christians in 1 Corinthians 14:26–33. It is highly participative.

People who had allowed themselves to be dumbed down in pews found this kind of recovery of voice to be 'a nearly new phenomenon'. It characterised the recovery of the vitality of faith. Jan Kofran, in 1999, reflected:

Sharing the common life of the community of baptised is one of the most important characters of the Community. People gathered in it had to learn to take responsibility for different roles in the church.

Things like free, spontaneous prayers were a nearly new phenomenon – if compared especially with the classical atmosphere of traditional-style Czech baroque churches. Also the liturgy in small groups, gathered somewhere in small apartments, was something entirely new. Bible readings and comments on them or homilies were provided in turn by any member of the Community … The Community prepared itself for the celebration of the Eucharist by everyday meditation on the biblical readings for the Mass of the Sunday to come. In addition this was also considered as a sign or expression of the unity of the Community …

A small group enables its members to 'bear one another's burdens' (Galatians 6:2). This has been practised both in relation to spiritual and to practical or material needs. The members of the Community have been sharing a minibus. Later they have bought a building of a more than 150-year-old school. The ruin of it has been repaired and reconstructed over 15 years till today. Common physical work of Community members is also of importance. The experience of 'common sweat' is unique and cannot be replaced by anything else.

The school building, situated about 60 km from Prague, is a place for meetings of the Community all round the year. One week of summer meeting is an important occasion for sharing problems, lectures and celebrating reconciliation. By this event, sharing troubles or experiences can be more organised. However, sharing has much to do with prayer, reconciliation and liturgy.

… the Eucharistic celebration takes place every two weeks. The Community is divided into five groups which, one after another, prepare the respective liturgy. Starting by choosing music and songs they prepare first of all the liturgy of the Word. One of them provides the introduction to the whole celebration. In that introduction also important events, feasts or anniversaries of Community members are mentioned. Another member of the preparing group is asked to introduce the readings. Also, the prayer of the faithful (oratio fidelium) and possibly other prayers have to be prepared.

The most important part of the preparatory work is preparing the homily. The members of the group compare several versions of translations of the readings, and share their opinions about the main ideas of the readings. A responsible moderator of the group is usually one of the ministers. The homily is given by one of the members of the group. He speaks, taking into account all the discussions of the preparing group. After the Eucharist celebration there is a sort of agape (that is, practically, the Sunday lunch). After lunch comes again a sharing: discussion of some topical questions, discussions with guests, sports, cultural activities, etc. Special attention is paid to preparing the liturgy of the Word for children. The liturgy takes place either in the apartments or in the working places of some of the members (e.g. schools). This is not only an old tradition, but it must be half official because of its not having been recognised as an act of the Community by the hierarchy!

A special importance has been given to preparing Holy Week and Paschal Tide. In Holy Week there is also renewal of the vows of the ordained and people in other orders.

The development of celebrating the Sacrament of Reconciliation is of special importance. First of all, preparation for the celebration has been traditionally based on biblical readings. In the Czech parish churches this is not always observed. For so-called 'pastoral reasons' classical anonymous confession is practised. This happens in spite of the fact that the respective manual with the selective text or readings has been in existence since 1982.

Open confession in the groups (for practical reasons the Community is divided into three groups for celebrating Reconciliation) became common. Step by step, open confession of one's sins is practised. Thus the participants can support and understand each other better. However, such a form needed to develop over many years to create an atmosphere of trust. At the beginning, an individual meeting with the presiding priest after the common confession was obligatory. This created time for additional confession of sins which the penitent did not intend to confess openly. Gradually, however, this requirement was relaxed. Having confessed one's sins, every penitent suggests his sign of reconciliation (penance) to be accomplished/approved with the help of other participants. The atmosphere of the celebration is not that of a discussion. Nevertheless there is a chance for sharing and supporting each other. The dialogue is mostly between the penitent and the presiding priest; however, the other participants can share the feelings or suffering of the penitents.

Of special importance is the Reconciliation celebration which takes place at the end of the one-week summer meeting. The foregoing days are used for preparing face-to-face reconciliation between the members of the Community. Such couples can, in their individual talks, sum up their relationships during the whole year. Thus the atmosphere of interpersonal relationships can be cleansed.

Also children and teenagers are gradually introduced into such a way of celebrating reconciliation …

THE CZECH REDISCOVERY OF FULL PARTICIPATION IN LIFE AND WORSHIP

One of the great contributors to the life of the Iona Community in the early years was Ralph Morton, its deputy leader.

Through the vision of Ralph the need for members to meet in small house churches, called family groups, was recognised. These provided an early (the earliest?) sign of a worldwide development of basic ecclesial communities. In them members can go deep into the faith and deep with one another. Thus they can contribute to plenaries and to Community Weeks on the island of Iona, and receive in return the insight, criticism, strengthening of other members on their different journeys. We are to be 'no more children but grow up into Christ'! How bring this about? The level of parish gatherings does not offer great opportunity for people to get deep in matters of the faith. This is especially the case with the shy and doubting who often give up on the church. In contrast, in small communities of 8 to 10 people, they can get confidence to share their thoughts, find where others stand and seek the truth together with them. The growth in confidence allows them then to contribute and receive in larger gatherings, in congregations and assemblies. Given voice and place in the small communities, they can then contribute to the church's total growth.

When Margaret and I left Scottish Churches House in Dunblane to work in Geneva, some people told us, 'We have been able to stay with the local church, where we are treated like kids, only because when we have participated in events at Scottish Churches House we were treated as adults.' In Czechoslovakia the necessity to keep out of sight of the secret police forced people to meet clandestinely in small groups. They found they had to become adults in faith – to do for themselves what they had previously expected clergy to do for them. Now the clergy were with them in the underground on the same footing! One of the testimonies the Czechs gave was that when people who had been accustomed to the traditional church joined a group for a house Mass, they found all the familiar indicators as before – but were quite taken aback by the extent of the participation of members. In learning to make their different contributions members grew in faith and life.

All churches agree in theory that the definitive ministry along with Jesus Christ's is that of the whole people of God. How can God's people make impact on the world if they are 'treated like kids' – told how to live instead of discovering that with others, and growing in faith and life in that process?

Czechs point the way. It meant designing a participant church with members contributing according to their gifts and different experiences.

Faith rooted in life

Clergy in the hidden church did not wear special clothes.

They worked for their living, earned their keep.

They were free to marry. Celibacy was a particular calling, not a required one.

They preferred to celebrate Mass in homes rather than in cathedrals.

They believed that ordination services for priests and consecration services for bishops were better held in workplaces than in cathedrals. That made more impact.

The common factor in all these points is the conviction that the ordained should not live lives separate from the rest of the church membership, but be closely related to them. They thus made:

a biblical point – that the church is built up by all the limbs and organs playing their part as in Ephesians 4.

a theological point – that the ordained are not a special category of Christian but only Christians with specific assignments.

a structural point – that any patterns of church life that are layered in such a way that the living experience and faith of the members get lost en route are fatally flawed.

an ecumenical point – that church unity does not have its focus in particular ecclesiastics, but in the body itself: 'In fact, God appointed each limb and organ to its own place in the body as he chose … there are many different organs but one body … God has combined the various parts of the body giving special honour to the humbler parts, so that there might be no division in the body but that all its parts might feel the same concern for one another' (1 Corinthians 12:18–25). The best theological statement which I came across in this matter was not in words. It occurred in the Indian congregation in Guatemala already mentioned. The priest came in wearing ordinary clothes and his robes over his arm. He put the robes on in front of the congregation. He conducted a service in which prayers were invited from the people, who responded with confessions, thanksgivings and intercessions. He developed a dialogue sermon with them on the basis of the day's biblical readings. After the benediction he went to the door, took off the robes in front of the congregation and went out. This formed an unspoken statement: He was a member of the church, given a particular assignment, after which he resumed his ordinary membership.

Jan Kofron traces the development of wider assumptions of responsibility in the hidden church:

In spite of some democratic elements, the Community was, at least to some extent, priest-centred at its beginnings. Note that those who were leading were also much more threatened. The authority of bishop was without any exaggeration linked with danger of death. This, for example, was why one of the bishops, after his being nominated, burst into tears. A phenomenon such as crisis of authority practically did not exist during the time of Communist oppression! One could quarrel or disagree with opinions or attitudes of his bishop, but a bishop as such was always honoured.

However, after the revolution of 1989 more democratic elements came to mark the leadership of the Community. The leadership of the Council at first consisted of all the ordained men plus two other Community members, who were elected. Now such a system has been left behind. All the members of the Council are elected. The Council is responsible for planning all activities of the Community, such as liturgy celebrations, theological studies and courses (for adults, youngsters and children), spiritual exercises, summer meetings, rebuilding the meeting centre, inviting guest professors and other personalities from abroad, etc. The Community has been editing an internal journal for its members called RATOLESTI (SPRAYS) where all announcements about the life of the Community are published.

In general, today's Community is striving towards a 'communio' church model. Exclusive leadership by one man could have some advantages in the period of persecution. In that time it was simply much more practical or safe to be involved as little as possible. Everybody knew what for him was necessary to know. Nowadays the situation has changed and people participate fully in decision making.

It is important to add that the Community always has been a community of leaders – leading other communities themselves. Thus there was a sort of multiplication effect.

After the Velvet Revolution, the openness of the community could be broadened out because of the disappearance of existential danger. This was why it started to be opened especially to the people on the fringes, to those who, in spite of their seeking, could not find a home in the traditional church. However, the Community was not a sort of ghetto during the Communist regime either. Nevertheless it took at least one year of candidature before any new member would be admitted. The candidature implied a singular contact with one community member over a one-year period which was spent in many face-to-face discussions, prayers, sharings, etc. After such a screening, and consultation with the rest of the Community members, the candidate would be recommended for membership. Today such a screening is not necessary any more, but the stability or equilibrium of newcomers is not always the very best! Thus such a security measure had a good side effect as far as the quality of newcomers was concerned. This was also why not many newcomers from the time of the 'ancien régime' left the Community.

(Jan confided to me that the stratagem of attaching a probationer to a trusted member for a year proved so effective in producing mature, committed members that it might be used as a normal discipline for 'apprentice Christians'.)

AN EDUCATED MINISTRY

'Stop thinking like children! With regard to evil be infants, but in your thinking be adults.' (1 Corinthians 14:20)

Jan Kofron observes:

Very soon, after having started its first activities, the Community realised that theological studies for everyone were indispensable. Goodwill and enthusiasm were not sufficient for an independent existence under Communist oppression. Therefore there were courses of bible studies, systematic theology, moral theology and other basic disciplines, given especially by professors who were not allowed by the regime to teach officially.

The studies were attended by about 80 percent of members (both men and women). Later, the texts for courses for theological formation from Wurzburg, released by the German Bishops' Conference, were smuggled into Czechoslovakia and translated into Czech. These became main textbooks for clandestine seminars.

During the Communist occupation, normal social and political action was impossible. The need not to make themselves known to the secret police meant that Charter 77 (the claim for human rights issued by intellectuals including Václav Havel) could not be signed, to the great regret of the members of the hidden church. That would have identified the membership to the secret police.

Yet for theology to justify its name, engagement as well as scholarship is needed. So what kind of involvements were undertaken once the Velvet Revolution took place?

Jan Kofron writes:

The Community seemingly does not have any outward programmes in the social or political sphere. It is a spiritual centre having as its only aim a mature response to Jesus and his challenging message. Such a spiritual rooting enables the Community members not to trim their evangelical radicalism. Everybody gives his response to the challenge of the Gospel according to his abilities and gifts. Of course this does not mean that such questions would never be discussed by the Council of the Community!

Community member Jan Klimes clarifies further:

The Community as a whole works out a background on the basis of which members decide on their personal involvements. The Community as a whole does not act as a unit in engagements in society … Yet particular problems can be shared and should be. The Community should sustain the courage of the person by prayer. But it is the person in the situation who must judge how to act … I believe that we should be radical. That is, by derivation, being well-rooted. What is the root? Jesus! … That will not lead to abstract theological discussions but to practical action. We must take care not to lose our radical edge of Christian identity in struggles and demonstrations!

In Scotland, great emphasis has been placed on the need for an educated ministry. The concern has justification. If God's Kingdom of justice, truth and peace is to be established in this world, the ministry to the world has to be well-instructed and well-equipped. But while the concern is warranted it has been misdirected. Its focus has been on those of us who are ordained – whose ministry is auxiliary. It is the ministry of the whole church which needs to be mature and well-furnished through perceptive use of the gifts of the Spirit distributed throughout. At times and in places, 'little-educated', illiterate people may be the vanguard, for when we speak about growth in Jesus Christ that does not have to do with formal education and expertise. There are many ways in which the whole people of God can be resourced for ministry in the world.

Theology is principally a lay activity. It develops from the relating of God's will and purpose to situations we face in the world. Lay women and men live more closely to life's pressure points. They have a basis denied to those scholars who are confined to desks and work within walls. Scholarship is an essential contribution to theology. But those of us who are scholars need to be engaged where it matters if we are to do theology of significance.

The Czech clandestine church unerringly identified an essential feature of church. It concluded that theological studies for everyone were indispensable. This is a sign of the kind of church which Paul envisages when he pleads that we be no more children, but grow up into Christ.

Jan Kofron continues:

After the November revolution of 1989 the Community could make use of the new freedom and it was possible to start with more open activities. It became obvious that, especially under new conditions, the only way to witness to one's Christianity was based on an ecumenical approach. Though there had been some ecumenical contacts in the past, the extent of them was very limited (caused by the danger linked with such activities). After a short reflection on possibilities, the Institute of Ecumenical Studies, Prague was founded.

The Institute's goal is to provide a theological education and ecumenical formation for responsible Christians who, in addition to their secular jobs, want to contribute to the rejuvenation of the present church and society. The graduate, who is anchored in her/his own church, should be able to lead qualified ecumenical dialogue and perceive the needs and wounded spots of her/his changing society. Therefore, this study is conceived as a minor subject to a major one studied at a different college. The median age of students is 28 years, and 36 years that of the professors. Both students and professors are representative of five churches. There are about 50 students in the Institute (two-thirds Catholics). There are lawyers, economists, musicians, natural scientists, technicians …

The Institute was founded in 1995. At the beginning, most of the teachers were volunteers coming out of the former clandestine courses of theology. Practically only the director was full-time engaged and paid. The school was subsidised by several sponsors from abroad. Last year the Institute succeeded to be incorporated into the body of the Evangelical Theological Faculty of the Charles University in Prague. Its curricula were accepted for bachelor studies. At the beginning of each academic year there is a 10-day intensive residential course outside Prague, consisting not only of lectures and seminars but also of common spiritual formation – celebrating liturgies of various churches as well. Two times a year there are retreats. Once a year there is celebration of liturgy. There come also guest professors from abroad to participate on winter courses, with sport activities combined also with lectures. As the second activity of the Prague E.S. Community after November 1989, publishing is to be mentioned. People of the Community gave an incentive to founding an ecumenical journal of theology called GETSEMANY. Besides that, a small publishing house called SIT (i.e. NET) was founded. In the period between 1995 and 1999 about 20 books were published.

As has been noted, I was in touch with basic ecclesial communities in Hungary while these were still in the underground. Once the Velvet Revolution had taken place and they emerged from clandestinity, it was found that they numbered 6,000. Approximately 5,000 of them were Roman Catholic and 1,000 Protestant. Many did not even know of the existence of others since they had to keep a low profile to evade the secret police. They formed themselves into five networks. I was present at the first one-day gathering of representatives in Budapest. It was ecumenical in both senses. It was concerned for the *oikoumene*, the whole inhabited world, seeking to discern how to fulfil social and political responsibilities which had been denied members while they were prevented by the police state. At the same time, it brought them into a *communio* in which people from different Christian traditions rejoiced to go forward together as collaborators with Jesus Christ in the work of the Kingdom.

In 1984, Margaret and I had taken eleven people from Britain to Italy to visit basic Christian communities, from Milan in the north to Naples in the south. We found that the inclination to develop life ecumenically came to them naturally. Even in situations where there were no Waldensian or Methodist counterparts, Roman Catholics would both appreciate their own tradition and move into a wider understanding of church.

In Scotland, we have Action of Churches Together in Scotland and Scottish Churches House, a base for cooperating churches. This resource is in place and would be able to sustain further ecumenical advance whenever churches get round to dealing ecumenically with Kingdom concerns which all of them share, and should they ever get round to common regional and national synods and assemblies.

In a time of tight finances the primary claim on available resources should be maintaining the ecumenical witness of churches together.

Jan Kofron sums up:

1. The birth of the Community was entirely spontaneous.

2. The history of the Community: a movement from a priest-centred group towards a 'communio' model. The Community could thus recognise the charismata (gifts of grace) of its members, which was the way to develop indigenous ministries on all levels.

3. Repentance and reconciliation are, besides the Eucharist, the centre of Community life.

4. Social, environmental and political activities are not on the fringes but are 'logical consequences of living the Gospel'.

The oppression of the church has turned out to be a gift of the Lord who is God-with-us; of the Lord who, having overcome the closed doors of our pragmatically thinking hearts, stands in the middle of us saying, 'Do not be afraid'. Therefore the name of the message of the past is the hope lived in the church of communio. The situation of being threatened enabled us to receive such a message.

Nowadays we are threatened again. Only the danger is sometimes more hidden. However, the message for today is the same as it used to be. It is the peace granted by the Christ who has died, is risen and whose coming we are expecting with a mature hope. The joy of the Easter morning may well be mixed with uncertainty or some fear; but basically the joy and new hope of the Easter morning must again be the source of new life in the middle of a desert of market economy, unemployment, wars and whatever evil.

It is understandable that we would like to possess a recipe to deal with this. I do not know of any myself. I think even that, should we use words like 'the struggle' or 'fight for light', we should use them when fighting against any cheap recipes – fundamentalist approaches, etc. Ready-made recipes can be even dangerous. First we should cry with the blind: 'Lord, let us receive our sight!' (Mark 10:51). The following question should be: 'What shall we do?' (Acts 2:37). However, the response should be found in the garden of Gethsemane again. We won't be there alone, I believe. There our Lord will be on his knees – the same one who on the one hand is respecting traditions of his nation and religion but on the other hand is a friend of prostitutes, of tax collectors, of the poorest of the marginalised people of all.

The last Mass I attended before departure went thus: Bishop Fridolin presided, Bishop Jan at his side. The adolescents formed a band to lead hymn singing. A time of confession was announced and about half of the people present offered prayers (out of around 40 participants). About the same number were later to contribute intercessions. There was a responsive psalm. Bible readings came from members of the congregation. The New Testament reading was the responsibility of an 18-year-old girl who proceeded to give the sermon. The children, who had gone out for their own sermon-equivalent, rejoined the company for the communion. They brought the elements and the vessels to the table and removed them at the end. The bishops together gave the blessing. They had presided over participant worship very like that which Paul describes as being characteristic of New Testament times.

PRUNING BRINGS NEW LIFE

Dr David Barrett, Professor of Missiometrics and publisher of the *World Christian Encyclopaedia,* researches and assesses world trends in mission. In 2004, he reported that there were 20,000 movements and networks with a total of 394 million church members with the following features in common:

🌿 They reject historical denominationalism and restrictive overbearing central authority.

❧ They seek a more effective Christian lifestyle.

❧ They are very fast growing.

In the 95 countries I have visited since starting work for the World Council of Churches in 1969, I regularly sought contact with such movements and networks, especially with basic Christian communities. Sometimes these develop their lives within recognised church frameworks; sometimes the official church pushes them away. In the USA, where they are simply called small Christian communities (the description varies), the Lilly Endowment Inc. recently funded a three-year project to investigate numbers within the Roman Catholic tradition. 37,000 were identified. It was hazarded that, taking into account a proportion which could not be detected, there must be at least 45,000, with a million members. Of these, three quarters were parish-attached (in history this has been called 'ecclesiola in ecclesia' – 'wee church within big church'); the other quarter were on the frontiers of the official church.

But there is not only one road to church renewal. In every situation the challenge is to relate the revelation of God in Christ to the particular circumstances with which human beings have to reckon. That takes much prayer. It means persisting through times of setback. It can take years, not months, to turn things round. The biblical word 'patience' is apt. In normal parlance it often refers just to the business of enduring with gritted teeth. In the biblical word, a Mandela factor is added. God prepares secretly resources which will turn the situation round.

Endurance has active energy in it because, however long it takes, through it God's promise will be fulfilled in the end.

ROSYTH, SCOTLAND

If the impetus to change in the Czech situation was Communist oppression, in Rosyth it was a situation of breakdown.

Margaret and I arrived in Rosyth in 1948 to find that, in the period of the church vacancy, a short leet of possible appointees had been drawn up. But when those on the list arrived to find a congregation all at odds and a breakaway group meeting in the Co-op hall, they said 'no thank you'. A second short leet was drawn up with the same negative result. It was then that we were turned to.

Clearly, some fresh approach was needed. One of the gifts of breakdown is that people are desperate enough to try alternative ways of working. Once I had assessed the situation I concluded that the hope of moving forward lay in rooting the life of the congregation in the bible, starting with the kirk session (the body of representatives – at that time all male – who gave attention to the life, service and mission of the local church). I raised the matter at one of the earliest session meetings. The reply was gruff and decisive: 'That's not kirk session business!' After a month or two I tried again. This time it was grudgingly agreed to allow 10 minutes of bible work to start each meeting. Then half of the kirk session turned up with apologies 10 minutes late. With the others it was like getting blood out of a stone.

I persisted. At last God gave that precious gift: frustration. Mr Taylor, a painter in the dockyard, stood up. 'I'm fed up with this,' he said. 'It is neither one thing nor the other. I move that, for a year, we have half an hour's bible study to start our meetings, that all of us turn up for that, and if it doesn't work we kill it off at the end of the year.' This was unanimously agreed. Over the months which followed the members became so fascinated by the relevance of biblical text to the issues they faced in the dockyard that they did not notice when the year was up. It was about 18 months before the painter rose again.

'I got this all wrong,' he said. 'At first when I told the wife that the minister wanted us to do bible study, she said, "It's eleven o'clock at night before you come home as it is. If you do bible study as well it will be midnight!" It hasn't been like that at all. The bible itself has given us a better judgment on what matters. We now get rid in half a minute things which would previously have occupied half an hour. I move that from now on we have an hour's bible study to start every session meeting.'

This was unanimously agreed. The only problem after that was to stop them at the hour. Over the following years they became a biblically instructed resource for the whole congregation. If I had to be away, I could detail three elders to take each service – one responsible for the structure, one for the prayers, the third for the sermon and children's sermon. Sunday school teaching was enriched by their leadership. So many adolescents pressed in that four bible classes were needed to cope – and elders could be mandated to give instructed oversight to each. The younger elders related especially well to the young people.

'We dodged the difficult bit' (Rosyth Parish Church)

In kirk session meetings we did not follow a set lectionary but found our way to whatever part or parts of the bible were likely to illuminate our journey. Here is one instance:

We had spent an hour on Jesus' encounter with the epileptic boy when he came down from the Mount of Transfiguration. I observed that I felt that we had got deep into that incident and had shared perceptive comments from our own experiences.

An elder disagreed. 'We dodged the difficult bit.'

I came back. The experiences of prayer which we had shared, I thought, were fresh and full of insight.

'Aye, that was good,' he admitted. 'But it wasn't just prayer that was needed for the young lad to be cured, it was prayer *and fasting*. We did nothing about fasting.'

I responded again. When copies of the bible were made by hand the copier might occasionally slip in something which accorded with his own convictions. For instance, a monk who led a very austere life could have slipped in the words 'and fasting' even if the words were not there in the original text.

'It says *and fasting*,' was all that I got in reply.

I tried another tack. In the Middle East and in eastern countries there was a tradition of fasting which made it a far more natural part of life than it would ever be for us in this part of the world. Even if the words were original, they need not apply to every church everywhere.

'It says *and fasting*,' the elder insisted.

He would not budge. We had to agree that we would look into the subject next time and try to identify relevant scriptural passages. It was then that we discovered, thanks to that elder's intransigence, the marvellous reflection on fasting in Isaiah 58: that the reality of fasting is not in outward conformity or even in self-denial as such, but in self-denial which promotes justice: a fairer sharing of food and other resources which God has supplied for needs of the whole human family.

Meanwhile, Margaret, who was gifted with a marvellous mixture of grace and toughness, got the women sorted out. The Fellowship and the Woman's Guild were at loggerheads. She helped the Fellowship to see that there was no value in being biblically concerned if that had no relation to the way you lived in the world; the Guild to see that life in the world needed to be nourished and guided by biblical insights. Moreover, she helped both to see that a church was well served if it had bodies with both emphases working side by side!

Those who occupied offices in the church had also to be sorted out. It became clear that, as the situation had deteriorated, members who had the appropriate competences had given up, and others, out of the kindness of their hearts, had occupied the abandoned posts. If the church was to serve the world effectively, steps had to be taken to replace the Session Clerk, the chairman of the Congregational Board, the Sunday School superintendent, the chairperson of the Woman's Guild, the organist and the church officer. One of the hardest jobs I have done in my life was to go to these people, speak appreciatively of the concern for the church which had led them to volunteer for office, urge them to see that their gifts lay elsewhere and suggest that they demit their current responsibilities. Whether or not they were taken aback with such straight talk, they all offered their resignations and not one left the congregation. In one instance I did an outrageously revolutionary thing. When nominations for the Congregational Board produced one person's name I asked if there were any other nominations! That had not been done previously. The first name proposed was considered sacrosanct. It brought in fresh blood when further nominations were sought.

On one occasion a neighbour said to Margaret, 'Ian terrifies me!' 'I'm not surprised,' she replied, 'but in what way in particular?' 'Well, when new members join, he consults the elder of the appropriate district and the member, about their gifts, interests, spare time and so on, and they are given a part to play in the light of these.' 'So?' 'Well, then he just leaves them to get on with it!' 'And would they get on with it if he fussed round them like a hen round chickens?' asked Margaret.

Jesus meant us to take off from his life into new fields, guided by his living presence. He makes this clear in John 14:12: 'Anyone who has faith in me will do what I have been doing; he will do even greater things than these, because I am going to the Father.' As worship developed through history it took many forms. I had the advantage, during the twelve years in Rosyth, of having an evening service. The morning service, taken from the front, was characterised by a strong march of worship where people knew where they were at each point and could be engaged mentally throughout. The evening service offered scope for trying out different approaches. In particular, three forms may be mentioned, all of which required me to give out relevant texts for study about two weeks beforehand:

❧ There were bible study services, where I took the congregation through passages in the Old and New Testaments which gave contrasting or confirming testimonies.

❧ There were services in the hall where, at the point at which the sermon would usually occur, the congregation was divided into groups of six or eight to see what they had made of the biblical material in light of the life situations which they were facing; at the end of a period of discussion they shared insights and questions across the hall.

❧ There were communal sermons – where I took one of the biggest risks in my life. Communal sermons could only take place when there was some concern which affected the whole Rosyth community. Their work was overwhelmingly in the dockyard. Let us say that the concern addressed was one of the recurring threats to close the dockyard. Passages of the bible which I would give out beforehand would focus on the importance of work, respect which should be shown for different kinds of work and workers, payment for work adequate to sustain life, the kind of deprivation which was experienced when people had no jobs, etc. In the week leading up to the service, people would get hold of their neighbours: 'Come on, you have to help us understand how as Christians we should face the possible closure of the dockyard.' 'But I'm a Roman Catholic!' 'We need Roman Catholics.' 'I'm an atheist!' 'Good, we're short of atheists. C'mon.' About 140 people would come to the service, saying under their breath, 'He's not going to get me to speak.' At the communion table I would have four people, two on each side. They were there 'for starters', contributing two sentences each which had to lead from biblical insights to the realities which had to be faced. Then I held my breath!

In every case a thoughtful communal sermon resulted. Not only so, but members disciplined one another. If someone said something which interrupted the development, the next one might say, 'Look, we may get round to that point later on but first we have to do a better job on the matter we are dealing with.'

Tell me, what one-man/woman-band, however good, can compare with the richness of experience of different committed people seeking light for their communal path through prayer, bible study and the sharing of faith perceptions at the heart of worship?

One of the other activities which built up the church and blessed the community was the prayers for healing, which were held after every evening service. About 40 people would wait for these. They learned to be alert to needs around their doors and in the wider world, and to call the power of God into situations to restore and bless human life.

The maturing of Christians in Rosyth was illustrated by outreach. A Council of Churches was formed comprising Methodist, Baptist, Episcopalian and Church of Scotland representatives. Roman Catholics advised us, 'Don't worry if the priest won't play ball – he's even allergic to the company of his own people!' (How times have changed.)

We would do parish visitation together – a Methodist and a Baptist going down one side of a street, say, and a 'Piskie' and 'Presby' down the other. The only way of escape was to be a Roman Catholic or an atheist! For instance, if someone opened the door who said, 'You are Methodist and Baptist? – well, I am actually Episcopalian.' He or she would be told, 'No problem. We'll whistle over the Piskie who is just across the road.'

Our hearts in our mouths, we would set up a portable platform at the entrance to the public park on Sunday evenings and commend the faith to passers-by – who were very ready to gather round. Would the ordained from different traditions get into one another's hair? Would lay members and clergy be at odds? We made a great discovery: because denominational boats were buoyed up by such an immense sea of shared faith, the different testimonies merged into one commanding testimony.

We created a Council of Churches Platform. It meant taking over the local institute – a sign that what we did was relevant to the whole civil and industrial community (a church hall might have sent out too restricted a signal). Major world concerns were laid before the Rosyth community: the Central African Federation (using involved people who were little heard in Britain), nuclear weapons, apartheid in Southern Africa, the Suez crisis … The aim was not to sell a particular line or to get a 'church mind', but simply to encourage people to act on the basis of informed judgments. The Council also took up concerns about inadequate lighting and badly paved footpaths, carpeting the relevant Dunfermline town councillors.[19]

From time to time the Home Board of the church would address me: 'Don't you now need an assistant minister or a church sister or …' My reply would be some such response as: 'Over the last year, some eighty more people have become church members. A church which has 80 more ministers is hardly inadequately equipped for its task!'

The whole story of the twelve years of ministry to the ministers is set out in my book *Bible, Congregation and Community* published in 1959 by SCM Press. Some copies may be available in libraries.

Worship is the most important activity in which human beings can engage. It gets life into true perspective. Woven into its texture can be the anguish, fears, worries, doubts that human flesh is heir to – along with biblical insights, poetic imagination, testimonies to adversities faced and overcome, patient hope, love and joy. The range of life of the priestly people needs to find expression in worship. It forms a springboard of reality from which they can take off to transform the world in union with Jesus Christ. Today is a time for pruning – to bring forth fruit with perseverance. (Luke 8:15)

6.

ECUMENISM

In 1978, I was asked to do the preparatory paper on ecumenism for the Lambeth Conference of World Anglicanism, which is held every ten years. This broke with the precedent that only Anglicans were invited to do preparatory papers. The paper is given here.[20]

Prayer

Lord God,
whose Son was content to die
to bring new life,
have mercy on your church
which will do anything you ask,
anything at all:
except die
and be reborn.

Lord Christ,
forbid us unity
which leaves us where we are
and as we are:
welded into one company
but extracted from the battle;
engaged to be yours
but not found at your side.

Holy Spirit of God –
reach deeper than our inertia and fears:
release us into the freedom of children of God.

History is cut loose in our time. It is there for the making. We must use the word 'new' with great frequency. The world is on the turn and the church is on the turn. One can discern the Advocate at work, exposing our real state of affairs, pointing where sin, righteousness and judgment lie, bringing under question old patterns of living, accepted stances and relationships.

What is the ecumenical movement in this time but the whole inhabited earth rising with fresh determination to combat the chaos which continually threatens it in ever-new forms, and reaching out to a larger destiny; the whole inhabited earth lifting up its head, daring to have new hopes and aspirations; exposed, through them, to fresh sufferings?

In essence, the situation demands of the church two things: that it join the human race in its search for a more ample future, and that it point to the one from whom the hope and the promise come – living out the solid character of that hope and promise by being itself the first fruits of a great harvest. If the church is to accept the challenge of this time, it must be prepared for a modest role alongside all types and conditions of human beings; and it must live its testimony to the Trinity convincingly.

In a short paper, there is time to probe only one main question. The one I propose is: How is the church to handle a movement of this kind? All its instincts encourage it to reduce the problem to fit into compassable frames of reference with which it is familiar. The church's reaction at this point of history is crucial. In the light of its own conviction that the mystery at the heart of the universe affirms humanity, it has a quite peculiar responsibility for distinguishing, in and through the flux of events, signs of 'Kingdom stirrings', and for pointing to their source and substance in Jesus Christ. The church's instinctive reaction is to make Kingdom things church things, and then reduce them further to clergy things. When this happens, the understanding of the ecumenical movement suffers a sea change. It becomes the churches moving together in common enterprise and in new relationship. These common enterprises and the establishing of the new relationship occupy the centre of the stage. The groaning and travailing of the world towards rebirth takes second place. Commissions and committees are set up to fulfil these more limited purposes. They are dominated, virtually monopolised, by ourselves, the ordained. We then smuggle in, as if they were matters of substantial importance to humanity, our peculiar concerns, and reduce still further the horizons of faith.

This process is understandable, even if damnable. Every Kingdom thing threatens the church as it is. The ecumenical movement is at one and the same time the greatest hope which has appeared in the life of the church for centuries, and the biggest menace to its existing life:

❧ This Kingdom movement, by its very nature, splits the church on things which matter rather than promotes its unity on a lower plane. It forces the church to decide whether it is going, in the last resort, to affirm the Kingdom or to affirm itself. All over the world today, you will find one part of the church holding tight and trying to stay where it is, or seeking merely interchurch unity; while another part is intent on seeking God's Kingdom and his justice and letting the unity follow which flows from that. It is the business of the ecumenical movement to split the church, instead of leaving it settled in old conformities. The great promise of these times is where the church becomes a Kingdom sign of a new world order in justice and peace.

❧ The movement draws people out of denominational allegiances into new companies of venturing, and encourages them to invest time, money, thought, commitment in Kingdom rather than in church enterprises. So it is a hazard to the institutional church's very survival. Only a church which is prepared to lose its life to find it will welcome this withdrawal and redirection of its resources.

❧ It exposes the biblical text to the understanding of 'wise' and 'foolish'. The cultural, class and other assumptions – present but unacknowledged in traditional scriptural exposition – are being recognised. The basic hermeneutical principle is being re-established: access to true teaching is through *doing the will* of God. For this, careful scholarship is a valuable aid. But it is auxiliary not determinative. Marvellously fresh understandings of scripture are now being produced by peasants, industrial labourers, illiterates.

❧ It rejects the old skins and fashions new wineskins for the new wine. Forms of the church which have obtained for centuries no longer serve. That strong, centralised professional control exercised through hierarchy and bureaucracy, which Lenin also favoured for his own church, only cracks and splits when it tries to contain the ferment.

❧ It brings under question not only forms of the church as they have been, but its authority structures, ways of worship, styles and shapes of ministry.

❧ It produces crisis – it throws so many things most surely believed into the melting pot.

This is a bewildering situation for the church to cope with. As an institution, the church has a proper concern for continuity and respect for stability. These are real gifts, and are among the most important contributions that institutions can offer society. But this particular institution is meant to be a sign of God's transforming purpose, available to God for participation in mission, open to the changes which need to be brought about – and, in consequence, itself open to change and reshaping. The Bishops' Synod in Rome, 1974, saw the need to ' … render to the world a much broader common witness to Christ, while at the same time working to obtain full union in the Lord'. The Joint Working Group Report, 1975, stated that as the church sees the ' … possibilities of common witness, their search for unity will in turn advance. In the perspective of witness many of the problems which still divide them will appear in a new light.' As the church digs up the talent hidden in the earth and risks it in mission, joining God in a determination to bring the whole beloved world to its liberation and complete fulfilment, it will be clear what stumbling blocks of history and relationship, that are barriers to the little ones, have to be cleared out of the way. Not otherwise.

Whether the church will be prepared to engage in the ecumenical movement in its full range with full seriousness, or will seek to domesticate it, may be illustrated and tested by the way in which it does its work of theology, worship and ministry.

THEOLOGY

For most of its history, the church has treated theology as a reflection on its own life done for it by specialists. Now a larger task beckons: understanding the whole process of history under God, and redefining the responsibilities particularly committed to it as church. For this different work, it should be clear that scholars, specialists and professional theologians are, by their discipline, training and inclination, also theological cripples. Partly this is inevitable and partly it is reprehensible. Certain work of scholarship quite properly withdraws one from the points of pressure which the majority have to reckon with. If the limitation is appreciated, the task can be given its true proportion. The problem is where professional theologians still try to do the church's thinking for it. Two forms of theological withdrawal are reprehensible: from interaction with other disciplines, and from association with the people of God.

A substantial proportion of the church, at least in certain parts of the world, has the education to enable it to cope with all but specialist theological assignments. But that is not the main point. It is this: Only a whole body, variously gifted, distributed through the societies of the world, coming under different terms of pressure and opportunity, serving one Lord, can seek together to discern what God is doing in his world and to join God wherever opportunity offers. Theology in the end is a work of perception, into which all the other work of selection, investigation, research, evaluation is gathered. The Christian community, enlivened by faith, can draw upon the multiple resources and situations of its membership and contribute, through its hearing and seeing, to humanity's perception of life's significance and its open possibilities. That is the major work of theology. Only the theological community can undertake it. Relevant specialisms and technical knowledge can offer contributions which test and deepen insights. Should theology be thus understood, the following will ensue:

1. Humanity will begin to be reinherited

Theology will no longer present itself as a sectional interest, pursued by specialists, requiring a language course as an entry qualification. It will encourage all kinds of companies of human beings, seeking to reckon with life as it presents itself, to drive their questions deep into the mystery at the heart of the universe. Knowledge of God will no longer be the preserve of sacred circles. It can become the bedrock of meaning for all. Not only will atheists be compelled to rethink their theology (atheists are inescapably theologians, as they must make clear what kind of God or gods they reject); they are already doing so. The Spanish and Italian Communist parties, finding Marxist Christians at least as deeply and perceptively engaged in the struggle for a new society as others, are now arguing that the atheism of Marxism may be a peripheral matter, or may be a mistaken path – at any rate, it is not an essential part of dynamic Marxism (*Nuestra Bandera. Nueva epoca – No.85*).

2. The church will find itself reinherited

Class, cultural, racist, sexist assumptions, which have been smuggled into the theological statements presented as objective, will be identified and shown in their true colours. Peoples who have been disinherited by the power-drive and status impact of Western theology will come into their own – as they are, indeed, coming into their own. Theology will become the work of the world Christian family. Many new styles and approaches will need to be respected and received by those who had traditionally called the theological tune. Women, young people and children, industrial workers and peasants, literate and illiterate will play a real, instead of a token or marginal, part. They will prophesy, as Joel promised. Cultures and languages will bring their different illuminations. All this is just at its beginning – but what a tough and exciting prospect lies before us!

3. The commanding theological questions will get adequate attention

Secondary matters, such as the validity of orders, will be recognised as in-church concerns which must not be allowed to divert from Kingdom imperatives. The gospel will recover wholeness.

It is not haphazard that we are brought to birth – our contribution in the Kingdom is defined and delimited by the particular terms of life we are presented with. In our day, we placard theology as betrayal if it does not deal with ways in which (a) the image of God in human beings is being defaced (b) principalities and powers manoeuvre to get life to run their way, heedless of God's future for humanity.

When we do thorough work of research and biblical discernment on matters such as: the ownership and use of land, of minerals and oil, of the means of production (especially concentrating on the power wielded by transnational corporations); trade and investment policies; nationalism; the spread of military regimes and the spectacular growth of the armaments business; forms of personal and social alienation; the deep-seated basis of class, race, sex discrimination; medical technology and genetic manipulation; the creative responses met at all levels of life, which illustrate how human beings can live beyond themselves – we get into the fights God is engaged in and thus discover, together, God's ways, God's mind, God's provision. Then, with the aid of scholars, we can contrast and compare notes in the communion of saints.

In some places where at least a part of the church experiences the furnace of suffering, those things, which many of us have separated, are fused in the heat. Gospel wholeness is regained. Mrs Trinidad Herrera, of the Philippines, the squatters' choice as chairman of ZOTO – aware of the political and economic factors which her people had to deal with and their need to organise to claim a stake in life – answered my questions regarding the terrible torture she underwent. She spoke of the presence of God in a nightmare world of pain, God's sustaining, and her determination to continue to do God's will, whatever the consequences.

4. Engage in Kingdom enterprise – then you get Kingdom insights

Instruments must be forged which help Christian people to get purchase on life at these points, give them confidence for the work they have to do and train them in skills to play their part. People together will find some of the tools they need. But there must also be a conscious investment of resources to retool the church for world mission, for participation in this drive to a new world.

WORSHIP

One of the Church Fathers (was it Gregory of Nyssa?) said: 'If you are a theologian, you will pray; and if you pray, you are a theologian.' Prayer and worship demand deep probing reflection upon experience in light of the testimony of scripture. So those who pray and worship in sincerity and truth are building up theological resources (whether they would be classed as educated or uneducated).

The reality of worship and prayer is not found in abstraction from life but in engagement with the kingdoms of this world, in light of the promise that they will become God's Kingdom. It is the whole world which is to be brought in and spread out before God when the people assemble, as Hezekiah spread out his letter. It is sin in all the dimensions in which it thwarts God's loving purpose, small-scale and large-scale, which is to be confessed. It is the whole field of the world which is to be irrigated by forgiveness, offered up with hope and expectation, entered into by a company prepared to present their bodies as 'a living sacrifice'.

Where worship is done for people, or where they are offered only stage-managed forms of participation; where the concerns of the people are not expressed in their language and made the substance of prayer and praise – then what happens is, in the end, alienating. The great difficulty of the traditional leadership is really to believe that worship is the work of the people, the gifted people of God; that their endowments of the Spirit and many ministries demand outlet in prayer and praise as well as in service and prophecy. There is no need for fear. The moments of worship must have a blood relationship to the rhythms of life. The Faith and Order conference in Montreal distinguished seven moments of Eucharistic worship which could be accepted by all the churches that were present. Lay people, given freedom to develop acts of worship at Scottish Churches House, Dunblane, might stand the accepted pattern on its head, plunge straight into intercession, and finish with confession, forgiveness and adoration. But the confession and absolution would have richness and depth denied it when it is so quickly disposed of at a beginning of a service; and all the moments would be there – a feel for them is in the blood.

Again, skills need to be learned for handing back to people what has been taken from them. In a country like the UK one of the gifts of black-led churches is a spontaneity and participation of the members which can instruct churches that have become wooden.

Worship in the ecumenical movement draws upon the involvement, sacrifice and imagination of all who are engaged where God is transforming life, in family, neighbourhood, national and international environments; and through them lifts up a groaning and travailing creation.

MINISTRY

Acts of prayer and forms of worship disclose unwittingly the extent to which they are genuinely ecumenical or church-domestic. Where ecclesiastical dignitaries are first prayed for, then the categories of the ordained, then the ordinary people, a tale is told. It is arguable that very many churches in the world, including those which would totally reject the Roman Catholic model, act as if they believed in a category of ordained ministry or priesthood which is separately constituted, has its own internal validation, and acts in a top-down way. Not only is this nonsense in light of the ecumenical movement – which calls for resources which are much more the province of laity than ordained. It is nonsense in terms of almost every statement now being made about the church, whose direct participation in the ministry of Jesus Christ, whose furnishing with gifts of the Spirit, whose manifold servant availability is being recognised in word. It is implementation which has to catch up with profession. Time and time again, statements which seek to do more justice to the ministry of the whole people of God experience a slide, and bed down on the preoccupations of the ordained. What else can be expected when the trade union of the ordained is in full control of statements issued?

The laity are there to be cared for and cajoled out of apathy; for heads to be shaken over their stubborn refusal to pick up prescribed initiatives? If people do not come alive, could it be that we clergy are just too thick on the ground for the people to have space to exercise their ministry? Could it be that we are too fearful of breakdown to trust the Spirit? We must ask most seriously: where have we become stumbling blocks, put in the way of the little ones, inhibiting them in their exercise of ministry in the world?

The call for more vocations to ordained service can be simply one for the provision of further stumbling blocks. Only in light of the exercise of the many ministries can it be asked whether professional, ordained forms are required or not, and where and for what purpose they are needed. They must always be clearly auxiliary to the main ministry of the whole people.

When it comes to their deployment, the African *indaba* model, in which everyone participates and builds up decisions to a point where either one person or a group expresses the mind developed through the whole process, must now prevail instead of the top-down pyramidical model. But many forms of ministry are emerging in the World church today under the pressure of the Spirit, and are there for our instruction. They have developed, not from past patterns – though they relate to signs in the church's history – but from participation in the ecumenical movement of the whole household of humankind towards a fulfilment whose substance they discern in the biblical promise of a new heaven and earth.

THE CHALLENGE

We are called and empowered to live resurrection. We can face the reality of this world as believers (fatalists will say 'any system you substitute will be as bad as the one you have got'). We can live in the confidence that Easter brought and brings:

> The Lion of Judah
> flames out
> on the desolate band
> from his ambush of joy –
> ravished,
> slain to life,
> sing:
> 'Nothing, nothing,
> nothing, nothing, nothing
> now can destroy.

To believe in God the Father is to believe that someone is in charge who sees the whole game. This should provide enough confidence to allow us church people to be prepared to see developments go out of our hands – without that meaning they become unfruitful or bring chaos. The insistence on having a controlling agent, like a Communist Party or a Curia or a bureaucracy, is a sign of unfaith (in processes of history, or in a Father of all). Episcope, the need at many levels to keep an eye on developments, test and relate them, is a different matter. Means to exercise it must never degenerate into instruments of control.

To believe in Jesus Christ is to be confident that, from a position stripped of power and privilege, we can successfully (though it may be, in the end, over our dead bodies) confront the massive and commanding powers of the world and help to make them serve the purposes for which God brought them into being.

To believe in the Holy Spirit is to believe that people can find resources in themselves beyond all expectation, sprout capacities to handle life, surprise themselves and others by what they can accomplish, and thus 'bring the house down', gaining the applause of the Universe (Romans 8).

NOTES

1. From *Letters and Papers from Prison*, Dietrich Bonhoeffer, edited by Eberhard Bethge, translated by Reginald H. Fuller, Fontana, London,1959, p.124.

2. Too often Cardinals, Archbishops, etc, whom the media consult, answer out of a presumed competence, instead of directing enquiries to the point in the church where serious work on the subject is being done. (I see virtue in having Moderators who are appointed for one year only. That leaves media to identify where the real work is being done.)

3. In the dying days of his regime, Fidel, being quite obsessed by the hostility and interference of the USA, seems to have 'lost it'. Amnesty International reports 89 journalists jailed in Cuba since 2003. A sad ending.

4. The principle of reception tests guidance given 'from above' by whether it makes sense on the ground to people of faith.

5. Paul says in 1 Corinthians 9:5: 'Do we not have the right to be accompanied by a believing wife as do the other apostles and the brothers of the Lord and Cephas?'

6. From *Four Quartets*, East Coker, section IV, Faber, London, 1944

7. Scottish Churches Open College – Over the 18 years of its existence, the Scottish Churches Open College (SCOC) provided ecumenical theological education through a variety of part-time programmes. These programmes were designed to enable those who may not have been pursuing ordination to develop their theological understanding in order to contribute to the overall resourcing of the church in its widest sense. Through residential workshops, regionally based tutorials, and supervised placements, students learnt the rigours of theological study and the challenge of integrating their learning into their own context. Those who participated in the programmes went on to become youth workers, worship leaders, preachers, counsellors and community workers. Some did subsequently choose to opt for ordination or service in a specific office of the church (e.g. as deacons or parish assistants). In total, around 3,000 people participated in SCOC programmes over the course of its lifetime. Supported by all the major denominations in Scotland this was a unique, innovative and forward-looking theological resource, even if it proved to be relatively short-lived. (from Jayne Scott)

8. Scottish Churches House came into being through the enterprise of representatives of seven churches and some ecumenical bodies in the 1950s. Churches wanted a base for common thought and action, and looked for a house of hospitality and outreach rather than an ecumenical headquarters or some such alternative. Over the years they considered about ten buildings in different parts of Scotland and concluded that the buildings were unsuitable or not readily accessible. In the end, a ruined row of eighteenth-century houses in the Cathedral square in Dunblane were restored for this purpose. During a visit by its central committee, the World Council of Churches dedicated the enterprise in 1960; and in 1961 the House itself was dedicated and became operational. For enquires and bookings: Scottish Churches House, Kirk Street, Dunblane, Perthshire, Scotland FK15 OAJ www.scottishchurcheshouse.org reservations@scottishchurcheshouse.org

9. The Mungo Foundation – See www.themungofoundation.org.uk

10. The Iona Community – See www.iona.org.uk

11. From *The Tablet,* 14th August 2004, p.18

12. Eden Project – See www.message.org.uk

13. Centre for Human Ecology – Centre for Human Ecology is a Scotland-based organisation carrying out action, research and education for personal development, ecological sustainability and social justice. (From the Centre for Human Ecology website www.che.ac.uk)

14. From 'Epistle to a Young Friend', by Robert Burns

15. Extracts from Didache II from *Acta Sanctorum Ordures Sancti Benedicti,* 9 vols, 1668–1701, vol 2, p.7, chief compiler, Achery.

16. The extracts from *A Chain of Error in Scottish History,* M.V. Hay, Longman, Green & Co., 1922, p.210-231.Quoted in *Celebrating Saints: Augustine, Columba, Ninian,* Ian M. Fraser, Wild Goose Publications, 1997, ISBN 0947988890.

17. In his encyclical *Ut Unum Sint: On Commitment to Ecumenism,* Pope John Paul II asked other Christian communities to accord a status of primacy to the papacy, to lead Christians towards ultimate unity.

18. The Church of Silence (Ecclesia Silenti) – some Czechs speak of 'the hidden church'.

19. This led to an approach to me to stand as a councillor in the Labour interest in the major borough of Dunfermline, of which Rosyth was a part. I served as Streets and Lighting convenor for 5 years. One of my best memories when we left Rosyth was of a message from the local Tories passed on to me by Mr Kyle, a Tory elder. They wished us well for the next stage of life. They said they had been encouraged by my showing my colours publicly, and that it had inspired them to be more decisive in showing theirs. They particularly appreciated that it was political responsibility I had urged on church members from the pulpit, not a party line.

20. Essay first published in *Today's Church and Today's World*, CIO Publishing, London, 1977, ISBN 0715145606

THE IONA COMMUNITY IS:

- An ecumenical movement of men and women from different walks of life and different traditions in the Christian church
- Committed to the gospel of Jesus Christ, and to following where that leads, even into the unknown
- Engaged together, and with people of goodwill across the world, in acting, reflecting and praying for justice, peace and the integrity of creation
- Convinced that the inclusive community we seek must be embodied in the community we practise

Together with our staff, we are responsible for:
- Our islands residential centres of Iona Abbey, the MacLeod Centre on Iona, and Camas Adventure Centre on the Ross of Mull
  and in Glasgow:
- The administration of the Community
- Our work with young people
- Our publishing house, Wild Goose Publications
- Our association in the revitalising of worship with the Wild Goose Resource Group

The Iona Community was founded in Glasgow in 1938 by George MacLeod, minister, visionary and prophetic witness for peace, in the context of the poverty and despair of the Depression. Its original task of rebuilding the monastic ruins of Iona Abbey became a sign of hopeful rebuilding of community in Scotland and beyond. Today, we are about 250 Members, mostly in Britain, and 1500 Associate Members, with 1400 Friends worldwide. Together and apart, 'we follow the light we have, and pray for more light'.

For information on the Iona Community contact:
The Iona Community, Fourth Floor, Savoy House, 140 Sauchiehall Street,
Glasgow G2 3DH, UK. Phone: 0141 332 6343
e-mail: ionacomm@gla.iona.org.uk; web: www.iona.org.uk

For enquiries about visiting Iona, please contact:
Iona Abbey, Isle of Iona, Argyll PA76 6SN, UK. Phone: 01681 700404
e-mail: ionacomm@iona.org.uk